Short Bike Rides™
in and around
Washington, D.C.

Also by Michael Leccese:

Short Bike Rides™ in Colorado

Short Bike Rides™ in and around Washington, D.C.

Third Edition

by Michael Leccese

Revisions by Paul Thomas

An East Woods Book

The Globe Pequot Press

Old Saybrook, Connecticut

Photo Credits

Pp. vii,2: Bill Clark, courtesy of National Park Service; pp. 4–5: Fred Fizell, courtesy of D.C. Development Land Agency/National Park Service; pp. 16, 36, 88, 124: Paul Thomas; pp. 24, 114: courtesy of Historic American Buildings Survey; p. 30: Jack Rottier, courtesy of National Park Service; p. 42: courtesy of Northern Virginia Regional Park Authority; pp. 50, 64, 110: courtesy of National Park Service; pp. 70–71: courtesy of Library of Congress; pp. 76–77: © Charles Votaw; pp. 79: courtesy Montgomery County Historical Society; pp. 82, 86: courtesy of United States National Arboretum; p. 94: © Robert A. Ikeler Photography; p. 100: Paul Souders, *The Montgomery Journal;* p. 116: Charles Keely, courtesy of National Park Service; p. 126: Debra Ernst, courtesy of Arlington Country Government; pp. 134–35: M. Woodbridge Williams, courtesy of National Park Service; p. 138: Hugo Skrastins, courtesy of National Park Service; p. 142: Jeff Taylor, *The Montgomery Journal;* p. 152: Cecil W. Stoughton, courtesy of National Park Service; pp. 160–61: courtesy RTKL.

Library of Congress Cataloging-in-Publication Data

Lecesse, Michael.
    Short Bike Rides in and around Washington D.C. — by Michael Leccese : revisions by Paul Thomas. — 3rd ed.
        p. cm. — (Short bike rides series)
    "An East Woods book."
    ISBN 1-56440-893-0
    1. Bicycle touring—Washington Metropolitan Area—Guidebooks.
    2. Washington Metropolitan Area—Guidebooks. I. Thomas, Paul D. (Paul Dudley) II. Title. III. Series.
GV1045.5.W18L43   1996
796.6'4'09753—dc20   95-53719
                                                                   CIP

Manufactured in the United States of America
3rd Edition/3rd Printing

To Kathleen,
who rode twenty-three
straight days in the rain,
&
To Richard Ridley,
who taught me how to look at things

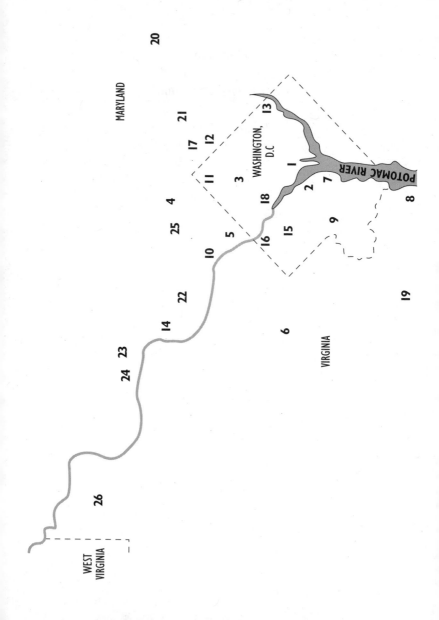

MARYLAND

WASHINGTON, D.C

POTOMAC RIVER

VIRGINIA

WEST VIRGINIA

Contents

Introduction

Washington, D.C., and environs are an urban cyclist's dream. The metropolitan area of 3 million people finds room for 48,080 acres of parkland and more than 670 miles of paved, off-road multi-use trails. The city and its suburbs have also designated 480 miles of signed on-road bike routes. And if weather turns foul, cyclists can (with a proper pass) jump on Metrorail, the region's 70-mile subway system, which sells bicycle passes good on evenings, weekends, and holidays.

Starting from the city's social and historic center, Georgetown, you could ride to Mount Vernon (16 miles); the foothills of the Blue Ridge Mountains (60 miles); Cumberland, Maryland (180 miles); or the Oz-like Mormon Temple (10 miles)—while hardly encountering a single automobile. Staying within city boundaries, you could visit the Lincoln Memorial, White House, Smithsonian museums, and U.S. Capitol, all within one hour of easy pedaling.

Not surprising for a city of political activists, Washington boasts the nation's largest bicycle club, the Potomac Pedalers, and its own two-wheeled transportation lobby, the Washington Area Bicyclists Association (WABA). In 1988 *Bicycling* magazine named D.C. one of the top ten U.S. cities for cyclists, who are served by more than a score of bike shops.

In *Captive Capital* (Indiana University Press, 1974) Sam Smith describes Washington as ". . . one of the most attractive, civil, interesting and pleasant [cities] in the country." Geography is part of what makes it so. Washington is located at the confluence of two rivers, where the coastal plain collides with the Piedmont foothills. Near the city line, the Potomac rushes over Class VI ("risk-of-life") rapids to meet estuary waters lapping up from the Chesapeake Bay. The old Federal City sits low on former swampland; the newer outskirts rise as high as 400 feet on bluffs overlooking the Potomac.

If Washington seems an anomaly among U.S. cities, perhaps it is because it is a planned city, founded by congressional fiat in 1790 and laid out by the brilliant, stormy French engineer, Pierre Charles L'Enfant. L'Enfant based his baroque street plan on elements of eighteenth-

I

century London, Paris, and Rome. Much of his vision survives: the broad avenues cutting diagonally across a grid of streets, the stunning vistas of monuments, and the abundant groves of trees.

L'Enfant conceived a diamond-shaped city 10 miles square, divided into four quadrants: Northwest, Southwest, Northeast, and Southeast. This can cause confusion. There is both a 1000 Pennsylvania Avenue N.W. and a 1000 Pennsylvania Avenue S.E.; there are two A Streets with near-identical addresses, four First Streets, and so on. In 1846 Arlington County and Alexandria reverted to the Commonwealth of Virginia, leaving the Potomac River as a natural boundary for the Northwest and Southwest quadrants.

Predating the founding of Washington were the eighteenth-century ports of Georgetown and Alexandria. Today these national historic districts are the focus of tourism. Both feature cobblestone alleys, colonial houses, cozy narrow streets, and excellent access by bicycle. You can still find one of the city's original boundary markers on Alexandria's edge.

Since 1966 the metropolitan area has been shaped by a new boundary that has effectively extended the city limits: the Beltway, a 66-mile superhighway looping around Washington. The Beltway can be a cyclist's bane, since it blocks many pedaling routes out of the city. This book will attempt to be your passkey through its concrete fortifications.

Freeways aside, D.C. has some of the nation's strictest zoning and planning laws. As a result of a 1910 law, no building may rise higher than twelve stories, or about 130 feet. Development near parks and public buildings is subject to review by the Fine Arts Commission. Here you find an asset rarely visible in Manhattan or even Pittsburgh: the horizon.

Culture in all of its forms enlivens life in the nation's capital. Easily accessible by bicycle are all the monuments, more than 150 embassies, the Kennedy Center, 70 museums, colonial historic districts, and restaurants ranging from Afghani to Vietnamese. As the city population is nearly 70 percent African-American, it is also home to a African-American university, several museums of African-American history and art, and landmarks such as Cedar Hill, the former resi-

2

dence of abolitionist Frederick Douglass, now owned and interpreted by the National Park Service. Moreover, there are Hispanic neighborhoods in Mount Pleasant and Adams-Morgan, a Vietnamese section in Arlington, and a vestigial Italian area downtown.

I've lived in Washington for fifteen years. During that span I've probably clocked more mileage on a dozen bicycles (from L'Enfant, an electric-blue ten-speed rescued from the trash, to Velo, an eighteen-speed touring model I once rode from Austria to England) than in my car. In general, life has improved for local cyclists during that time. For example, the National Park Service spent $1.5 million on an elevated path near Theodore Roosevelt Island, thus connecting two routes and creating one of the nation's longest contiguous bikeways. The 64-mile path connects Mount Vernon with the Blue Ridge foothills to the west.

Today, cycling in the Washington area seems poised for a breakthrough. Fed up with traffic and pollution, regional governments are weighing a $60 million plan to connect regional trails and lanes into a 1,000-mile system complete with standardized signs—a sort of interstate system for bicyclists.

This ambitious plan recognizes that a bicycle is an environmental tool. I hope readers will use this book not only for pleasure rides but also to plot rides to work, to run errands, and to visit friends and family. In some small way, you'll directly prevent pollution and ease the demand for more highways and parking lots. And yes, you'll save lots of money, too—fewer repair bills, insurance premiums, or payments for a second car.

That said, this region could be far more hospitable to bikers. And there have been setbacks. D.C. has eliminated the position of bicycle coordinator from city government. And the suburbs continue to sprawl with relatively little regard for bicyclists or pedestrians.

I urge readers of this guide to become advocates of bicycle transportation. Join the Washington Area Bicyclists Association and the League of American Wheelmen. Lobby your workplace to install a shower and safe bicycle parking. (Many offices already have a shower, installed long ago by some jogging exec. Ask your office manager to remove the old files so you can reclaim the space.)

Be sure that your local, county, and state representatives know you support bicycling. Find out what trails are on the boards and state your support for them. Here are two for starters: the Metropolitan Branch from Union Station to Silver Spring and the continuation of Capital Crescent from Silver Spring to Bethesda (the segment from Bethesda to Georgetown was completed in 1995). Build those two, and Washington has a Bicycle Beltway.

A word on safety

The biker looking to conquer the capital should take some precautions, such as the following:

1. **Wear a helmet.** Traffic here is insistent, swift, and sometimes abusive to cyclists. From 1970 to 1987, the number of cars in the area increased from 1.6 million to 3.2 million. If that's not reason enough, try this: Once someone tossed a bottle at my head when I was riding through the Adams-Morgan neighborhood. It struck my helmet and shattered. Without the hard hat, I'd still be picking shards of glass from my scalp.

2. **Buy the strongest U-shaped lock you can find.** Bicycles are more likely to be stolen than cars here. Be sure to secure both wheels and the frame to a fixture such as a bolt-down bike rack or a double parking meter. Better yet, bring the bike indoors or lock it in a parking garage.

3. **Carry maps.** The bikeways have been improved, but the rivers, train tracks, and freeways form many obstacles and dead ends. The city's quadrant system can easily confuse newcomers. All too often, meandering cyclists find themselves on four-lane roads or two-laners with blind curves and no shoulders. It isn't worth the risk, and there's usually a better way through. (The maps included in this book should help greatly. If you do veer off the routes, a good local map will help you get righted.)

4. Realize that off-road multi-use trails aren't for bikes alone. Despite common terminology, they are *not* exclusively "bike paths." Share them courteously with families out for a stroll, hikers, and in-line skaters, as well as other cyclists.

5. Take a buddy. Washington's violent crime problems have been well publicized, and while I've never felt afraid, I would advise cyclists to ride in pairs and carry spare parts and tubes.

About the directions

All rides include step-by-step directions and maps. Starting points can be reached by auto or Metrorail and are often near bike-rental facilities.

Some of the rides (23 and 24, for example) may be combined into longer routes. While some rides are planned as loops, others are one-way rides that require doubling back the way you came. In the latter cases, I've tried to include optional side-trips to historic or scenic sites that will vary the scenery on the return trip.

Rides 25 and 26 ("For the Pros") are longer and more challenging trips. Novice or out-of-shape cyclists should try the shorter rides first.

Local cycling clubs and regional park authorities can help plan rides. Most publish maps. Some even organize weekend rides. I've included a list of cycling sources in the Appendix.

Off-road cycling

If you bought a bike in recent years, chances are it was an all-terrain or mountain bike. For routes suitable for all-terrain bikes, see Rides 14, 19, and 23. When riding an ATB, take care not to trespass on hiking trails or disturb wildlife areas. As these types of conflicts increase, the National Park Service and other park authorities are banning knobby-tire bikes in many areas.

A word on climate

Washington's summers can only be described as torrid. The typical August mercury hovers around 95 degrees, with comparable humidity. Moreover, the summer air quality can be atrocious. During many summer days the pollution (most of it generated by the area's 3.2 million cars) makes exercise unhealthful.

The region atones for the intolerable summer season with lingering warm autumns and springs and mild winters. To wit, I tested most of the rides included in this book during a particularly sunny January with temperatures of about 50 degrees.

You can beat the summer heat by rising early to complete short rides before 9:00 A.M. Owning a bike pass for Metrorail also comes in handy. When the sun drops and the wind rises at about 6:00 P.M., I like to take off for Mount Vernon, timing the trip so I arrive at Alexandria's King Street station at about sunset. The air-conditioned ride home is particularly refreshing.

Monuments on the Waterfront

Distance:	13-mile loop
Approximate pedaling time:	90 minutes
Terrain:	Flat except for Arlington Cemetery
Surface:	Good paths, roads, and sidewalks
Things to see:	FDR Memorial, Tidal Basin, Hains Point, Jefferson Memorial, Arlington Cemetery, Lincoln Memorial, Korean War Veterans Memorial
Facilities:	Rest rooms, snack bars, and souvenir stands at the monuments and cemetery

This ride along the D.C. and Virginia banks of the Potomac River could take weeks if you savored all the riches en route. This is Washington at its most Athenian.

Start at the Harry T. Thompson Boat Center, where you can rent boats and bikes. If you are arriving by car and parking here, be aware of the two-hour limit in this lot. Head southeast on a bikeway that runs between the Kennedy Center and the Potomac River. Built in 1970 on the site of the Heurich Brewery, the 630-foot-long performing-arts center contains the American Film Institute movie theater, an opera house, a stage for major plays, a concert hall, a cabaret, and restaurants.

After riding past volleyball courts and through two narrow bridge underpasses (dismounting recommended), you will arrive in 1.3 miles within view of the Lincoln Memorial, at the John Ericsson Monument at Independence Avenue and Ohio Drive S.W. Carved from granite and dedicated in 1926, the Ericsson statue pays tribute to the designer of the U.S.S. *Monitor,* the ironclad battleship that changed the course of the Civil War.

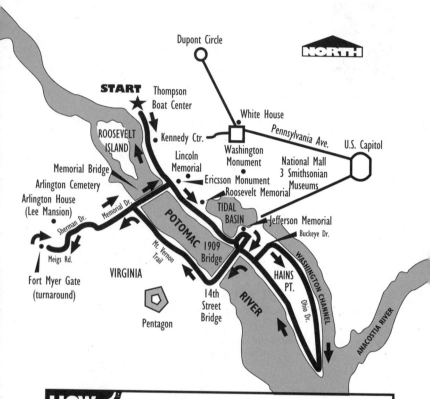

Dupont Circle

NORTH

START
Thompson Boat Center

White House

Pennsylvania Ave.

U.S. Capitol

ROOSEVELT ISLAND

Kennedy Ctr.

Washington Monument

National Mall 3 Smithsonian Museums

Lincoln Memorial

Memorial Bridge

Arlington Cemetery

Ericsson Monument

Roosevelt Memorial

Arlington House (Lee Mansion)

Memorial Dr.

POTOMAC

TIDAL BASIN

Jefferson Memorial

Sherman Dr.

Buckeye Dr.

Meigs Rd.

Mt. Vernon Trail

1909 Bridge

WASHINGTON CHANNEL

Fort Myer Gate (turnaround)

VIRGINIA

HAINS PT.

Ohio Dr.

14th Street Bridge

RIVER

Pentagon

ANACOSTIA RIVER

HOW to get there From north, Rock Creek Parkway south to Thompson's parking lot; turn right. From Mall, Virginia Avenue west across Rock Creek Parkway to Thompson's parking lot. From Virginia, Theodore Roosevelt Bridge or Memorial Bridge to Rock Creek Parkway to Thompson's parking lot. By Metro, Blue or Orange Line to Foggy Bottom/GWU, about a 1-mile walk or ride. From Metro station, walk south on Twenty-third Street (away from Washington Circle). Turn right on H Street, left on New Hampshire Avenue, and right on Virginia Avenue. Cross Rock Creek Parkway at crosswalk to reach parking lot of Thompson Boat Center. Follow one-lane road over short bridge to waterfront.

DIRECTIONS for the ride

- From Thompson Boat Center, right on trail heading toward Watergate apartments and Kennedy Center, Potomac River on right.
- Cross parkway intersection to reach path. Continue through outdoor volleyball courts.
- Ride (or dismount and walk) through two short bridge underpasses. Bear right with bike path onto Ohio Drive at Ericsson Monument.
- Proceed northeast for 0.8 mile on Ohio Drive past Roosevelt Memorial on left. Cross 1909 bridge. Turn right and follow signs to East Potomac Park (Hains Point).
- Cross under four bridges. Left at stop sign onto Buckeye Drive to begin loop of East Potomac Park.
- Right at stop sign onto Ohio Drive.
- At end of one-way loop, keep straight on Ohio Drive. Pass under four bridges. Do not cross 1909 bridge. Bear right toward Jefferson Memorial.
- Across from parking-lot entrance to Memorial, access Fourteenth Street Bridge bike path via curb cut on right.
- Cross bridge and bear right on bike path.
- Proceed upriver on Mount Vernon Trail past Lady Bird Johnson Park.
- To reach Arlington Cemetery bear left at fork in trail and cross George Washington Parkway three times at crosswalks marked with stripes.
- At Memorial Drive, stay on sidewalk. Detour to visitors center on left.
- At end of Memorial Drive turn right on Schley Avenue. Continue uphill via Sherman and Meigs avenues to Fort Myer gates. Turn around and return to Memorial Drive.
- Using Memorial Bridge sidewalk, cross to D.C. to Lincoln Memorial.
- Take unmarked road back to Ericsson Monument.
- Retrace path back to Thompson's.

View the Lincoln Memorial in profile and proceed downriver on Ohio Drive, with the polo fields of West Potomac Park on your left and the Tidal Basin beyond. (Time your ride for a summer Sunday afternoon if you want to watch part of a polo match.)

Washington's newest monnument, the Franklin Delano Roosevelt Memorial, will soon be a major attraction along this stretch of Ohio Drive. Scheduled to open in 1996, it will join the memorials to Washington, Jefferson, and Lincoln as major tributes to four great American leaders. Rather than a grand marble structure, the Roosevelt Memorial will consist mainly of a series of contemplative outdoor gardens.

Approximately 0.8 mile ahead lies a brief but graceful bridge stamped 1909 and ornamented with gargoyle fountains. Cross it and turn right at the circular flower bed to stay on Ohio Drive. Pass under four bridges for automobiles, Amtrak, and Metrorail, and then begin a 3-mile one-way loop around East Potomac Park, a popular picnic area that features an Olympic-size pool, a golf course, and many flowering trees.

At the park's apogee is Hains Point, fronting the confluence of the Potomac and Anacostia rivers and Washington Channel, a waterway full of pleasure boats. Across the channel lies old Fort McNair and its impressive brick buildings. The tall, domed edifice is Army War College, founded by Theodore Roosevelt after the Spanish-American War. National Airport is directly over the Potomac.

Hains Point beckons when you see huge fingers and a large bearded head rising from the ground. The startling figure is Seward Johnson's 1980 statue "The Awakening," which portrays a Brobdingnagian figure rising from the soil. Have your photo taken perched on one of the large aluminum digits, then proceed upstream, parallel to the Potomac River.

Return via the loop to the 1909 bridge. Instead of crossing, turn right toward the Jefferson Memorial. Built in 1943, this domed pavilion ringed by fifty-four columns houses a 19-foot-tall bronze statue of Thomas Jefferson and inscriptions of his words. The memorial fronts the Tidal Basin and its famous crescent of cherry trees, whose early-April blooms are cause for citywide celebration.

Returning to the parking-lot entrance, look for a curb cut leading to a bike path over the Fourteenth Street Bridge. The bikeway over the span is an engineering marvel—wide, smooth, and well-protected from the main roadway. You'll have views of the Pentagon, sailboats, and bridges carrying Metrorail and freight trains over the river. At the base of the bridge on the Virginia side, bear right onto the Mount Vernon Trail, which parallels the George Washington Memorial Parkway.

With the Potomac on your right and Boundary Channel on your left, pedal about 1 mile to Lady Bird Johnson Park. Designated in 1968 to honor the aboreal-minded First Lady, the island park is planted with 2,700 dogwoods and 1 million daffodils (carefully counted, according to the National Park Service). Just over the parkway (a dicey crossing for cyclists) stands Columbia Island Marina and the fifteen-acre Lyndon Baines Johnson Memorial Grove, planted with hundreds of white pine trees surrounding a memorial stone shaped from pink Texas granite. Continue on the trail a few hundred feet toward Arlington Memorial Bridge, dedicated in 1932 to symbolize the reunion of North and South. Bear left on the trail to avoid passing under the bridge, and ford two striped crosswalks across the George Washington Memorial Parkway. Cross a traffic circle to reach Memorial Drive, gateway to Arlington National Cemetery.

Ride on the sidewalk to avoid the macadam road surface. Pause to ponder "The Hiker," a 1965 statue dedicated to veterans of the Spanish-American War of 1898. The cemetery's visitors center is on the left, half-way down Memorial Drive. Lock your bike to one of the iron gates (no bike racks) if you want to go inside for information.

At the massive stone gate marking the end of Memorial Drive, turn right on Schley Avenue to make a short tour of the grounds. The route is well marked, as are roads off-limits to bikes. Continue up Schley to Miegs Avenue, which leads to the Lee Mansion high on a precipice with a view of the river and the monuments of Washington. This is a good place to park and explore the cemetery on foot. On the way back, visit a marker honoring city planner Pierre L'Enfant. This spot offers a magnificent view of downtown Washington. Then retrace your ride back to the Memorial Bridge.

Gingerly cross the traffic circle again to reach the bridge's sidewalk, which you can ride back to Washington. Pass by the enormous, golden equestrian statues and bear right at the end of the sidewalk. Again, carefully make your way across the traffic circle (preferably on foot) to the Lincoln Memorial grounds.

Built in 1922 to honor the author of the Emancipation Proclamation, the Memorial has since been a magnet for civil rights activism. Here, in 1939, black singer Marian Anderson performed her famous concert, defiant of segregation, and in 1963 Martin Luther King uttered his "I Have a Dream" speech to a throng of 200,000. Architect Henry Bacon designed the building in the style of a Greek temple with Roman detailing. Sculptor Daniel Chester French created the 900-ton figure of Lincoln from twenty-eight blocks of white Georgia marble. Beneath the Memorial lies a catacomb created by the construction. It's actually filled with stalactites and stalagmites formed by water dripping from the marble steps.

Flanking the Lincoln Memorial, and directly across from the Vietnam Memorial, is the site of the Korean War Veterans Memorial, a monumental landscape that features life-size-plus statues of soldiers marching across a reflecting pool. The memorial was dedicated in 1995.

Now you can either return to Thompson's or pick up the second leg of this monumental tour in Ride 2.

Monuments on the Mall

Distance:	9.7-mile loop
Approximate pedaling time:	90 minutes
Terrain:	Flat except for Capitol Hill
Surface:	Roads and paved paths
Things to see:	Washington Monument, Smithsonian museums, U.S. Capitol, Library of Congress, Union Station, the White House, Vietnam Veterans Memorial
Facilities:	Rest rooms, gift shops, restaurants, and bike racks at most museums

This tour combines the great houses of government with the great houses of knowledge. I doubt that even Manhattan could boast of such a concentration of cultural institutions and world-class landmarks.

Begin at the Harry T. Thompson Boat Center (bike rentals available), If you are arriving by car and parking here, be aware of the two-hour limit in this lot. Proceed to the Lincoln Memorial as described in Ride 1. Ride to the east steps of the Lincoln Memorial for a stunning view of an axis that includes the Washington Monument and, nearly 2 miles away, the U.S. Capitol.

Head down a slight slope past a souvenir stand on your right to pick up a path parallel to the 0.5-mile-long Reflecting Pool. Continue past the fountains (filled with mallard ducklings in spring) and jog to the left on the sidewalk to reach the pedestrian crossing at busy Seventeenth Street.

Pick up the path leading directly uphill to the Washington Monument, where a circle of flags always blows stiffly. This high ground is a favored spot for kite-flying. The cornerstone for the 555-foot-tall monument was laid in 1848, but the masonry structure was not completed

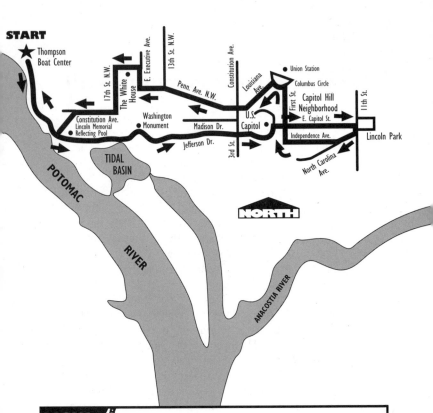

START

Thompson Boat Center

17th St. N.W.

The White House

E. Executive Ave.

13th St. N.W.

Penn. Ave. N.W.

Constitution Ave.

Louisiana Ave.

• Union Station

Columbus Circle

First St.

Capitol Hill Neighborhood

E. Capitol St.

11th St.

Constitution Ave.
Lincoln Memorial
Reflecting Pool

Washington Monument

Madison Dr.

U.S. Capitol

Independence Ave.

Lincoln Park

Jefferson Dr.

3rd St.

North Carolina Ave.

TIDAL BASIN

POTOMAC

RIVER

ANACOSTIA RIVER

NORTH

HOW to get there From north, Rock Creek Parkway south to Thompson's parking lot; turn right. From Mall, Virginia Avenue west across Rock Creek Parkway to Thompson's parking lot. From Virginia, Theodore Roosevelt Bridge or Memorial Bridge to Rock Creek Parkway to Thompson's parking lot. By Metro, Blue or Orange Line to Foggy Bottom/GWU, about a 1-mile walk or ride. From Metro station, walk south on Twenty-third Street (away from Washington Circle). Turn right on H Street, left on New Hampshire Avenue, and right on Virginia Avenue. Cross Rock Creek Parkway at crosswalk to reach parking lot of Thompson Boat Center. Follow one-lane road over short bridge to waterfront.

DIRECTIONS for the ride

- From Thompson's parking area, turn right onto bike path (Potomac River is on your right).
- Proceed 1.5 miles to Ericsson Monument. Turn left to head up short road (sign reads TAXIS ONLY) to Lincoln Memorial.
- Facing east toward the Capitol building, pick up bike path parallel to Reflecting Pool. Proceed 0.5 mile to Seventeenth Street pedestrian crossing (traffic signal).
- Take path short distance east (uphill) to Washington Monument. Proceed on bike/foot paths across Fifteenth and Fourteenth streets to Jefferson Drive. Begin tour of south side of National Mall.
- Follow Jefferson Drive about 0.5 mile along Mall. Right on Third Street and quick left on Maryland Avenue. Proceed past statue of James Garfield to U.S. Capitol grounds.
- Follow footpaths around south side of Capitol building to east front. Proceed to East Capitol Street. Pass through stone gates; left on First Street.
- Take First Street about 0.75 mile to Columbus Circle in front of Union Station. Turn right on circle and left into service road in front of station. Watch out for traffic in this busy area.
- Exit station area on service road; turn left. Take second right on Louisiana Avenue.
- Proceed less than 1 mile past parks and bell tower. Take oblique right onto Constitution Avenue. In two blocks turn right onto Pennsylvania Avenue.
- In eleven blocks, turn right on Thirteenth Street and quick left on Pennsylvania Avenue North. Pass National Theater and Willard Hotel to reach Fifteenth Street. Cross at signal to continue straight on Hamilton Place.
- In about one-half block, turn right through the gates onto East Executive Avenue. Exit through another set of gates; turn left on sidewalk past the White House. Walk bike to Seventeenth Street. Cross at Seventeenth Street signal and turn left.
- Ride three long blocks to Constitution Avenue. Cross at signal and pick up bike path (west) past Constitution Gardens and Vietnam Veterans Memorial.

- Return up Henry Bacon Drive to Lincoln Memorial. Return to Ericsson statue and retrace route to Thompson's.

Capitol Hill Detour: This 2-mile side trip through a Victorian row-house neighborhood takes you past the homes of many members of Congress. Be sure to stop at Eastern Market, an old-fashioned farmers' market at Seventh Street and North Carolina Avenue, for a late breakfast at Market Lunch.

From east front of U.S. Capitol:
- Straight on East Capitol Street, eleven blocks to Lincoln Park.
- Turn right on Eleventh Street.
- In one block, turn right on North Carolina Avenue.
- After stopping at Eastern Market, proceed on North Carolina to Pennsylvania Avenue. Turn right.
- Left on Independence Avenue at Second Street. Take first right onto First Street. Proceed five long blocks to Union Station to pick up the route.

North side of Mall elective: This route shaves several miles from the trip while affording a chance to see the Mall's other four museums: the National Gallery (East Building and West Building, featuring dramatically different collections), the Museum of Natural History, and the Museum of American History, which features an interesting selection of antique bicycles—not to mention a seminude statue of George Washington.

Directions from Jefferson Drive:
- Left on Third Street.
- Left on Madison Drive (one way).
- Straight on to Fourteenth Street. Cross to Washington Monument grounds.
- Straight to Seventeenth Street. Cross to path parallel to Constitution Avenue.
- Follow signs to Constitution Gardens and Vietnam Veterans Memorial.
- Follow path to Lincoln Memorial.

until 1884. From 9:00 A.M.. to 5:00 P.M. (until midnight in spring and summer), you can ride the elevator up to the 500-foot level.

Back on your bike, continue downhill past a souvenir stand on a path to Fifteenth Street. Cross carefully and take another path to a signal at Fourteenth Street. Dismount and cross to one-way Jefferson Drive, the starting point for a tour of the south side of the National Mall. Conceived by Pierre L'Enfant as a residential boulevard, the Mall was densely planted as a romantic forest in the 1800s and streamlined as a grassy, elm-lined promenade in the early 1900s. It is the home of nine Smithsonian museums plus the National Gallery of Art, an ice-skating rink, and a building of the Department of Agriculture. All museums are free.

Your first stop is the recently renovated Freer Museum, the first Smithsonian art museum, dating from 1923. Housed in a building styled after an Italian palace, the Freer collection devotes itself to Asian art, particularly jade sculpture, lacquers, and porcelain. Not to be missed is the ornate Peacock Room, which was moved intact from art patron Charles Freer's Detroit mansion along with more than a hundred artworks by James Abbott McNeill Whistler.

The next few hundred feet feature:

• the turreted Smithsonian Castle, a romantic brownstone structure designed by the architect of St. Patrick's Cathedral;

• the Arts & Industries Building, a High Victorian pile exhibiting American technology as it existed in 1876;

• the doughnut-shaped Hirshhorn Museum and its outdoor sculpture garden, both devoted to modern art; and

• the National Air and Space Museum, which is the nation's most visited museum (9.5 million people annually). Within this great hangarlike structure you can find everything from the *Spirit of St. Louis* to space modules used in the Apollo-Soyuz project. Almost everyone takes in a 70-millimeter IMAX film, shown on the Langley Theater's five-story screen.

If you stop to dawdle at the Castle, don't miss the Smithsonian's newest museums: the National Museum of African Art and the Arthur M. Sackler Gallery, devoted to Asian art. Both are located beneath a landscaped plaza facing Independence Avenue.

Continuing east, leave Jefferson Drive at Third Street to enter Maryland Avenue. On the right stands the U.S. Botanical Gardens, a Victorian-style greenhouse filled with tropical orchids and blooming cacti. Unless you take the shorter alternate route to see the Mall's north side (see "Directions for the ride" above), the next stop is what L'Enfant called "Congress House."

Started in 1793, burned in 1814, finished in 1867, and constantly updated since, the U.S. Capitol is situated on one of Washington's highest hills. In the 1870s it was landscaped by Frederick Law Olmsted, the principal designer of Manhattan's Central Park. The grounds retain odd little additions such as Japanese lanterns, a grotto, and a trolley stop. Follow a looping path to the Capitol's east side for views of the Library of Congress and the Supreme Court; then turn left on First Street. You will soon arrive at Union Station. Long empty and decaying, the 1907 station reopened in 1988 as a shopping mall after a painstaking $100 million restoration. Its Roman-inspired architecture matches that of just about any of D.C.'s great public buildings. Best of all, it still serves Amtrak, Metrorail, and commuter trains. Union Station features well-designed and well-located bike racks, so it's a good place to park the 18-speed and explore the city on foot or by rail.

After touring the grand station, exit the area via Louisiana Avenue, cutting diagonally southwest. Within four blocks, you'll meet Constitution Avenue. Turn right and in two blocks start coursing down the Avenue of the Presidents—Pennsylvania Avenue. Since the time of Thomas Jefferson, this 1-mile stretch has hosted the inaugural parade. Until recently, the street's seedy demeanor belied its importance. But a $1 billion effort since 1976 has resulted in four new parks and memorials, restoration of several major landmarks, and construction of new hotels, offices, and restaurants. On weekends the boulevard is lightly traveled. Don't miss the new Navy War Memorial, the Canadian Chancery, the National Archives, the FBI Building (open for a rat-a-tat of a tour), and the restored Old (1897) Post Office, with its 315-foot bell tower and pavilion filled with shops. At Thirteenth Street, Pennsylvania Avenue splits into North and South. Follow the ride directions until you reach a plaza anchored by a statue of Alexander Hamilton.

After one block, turn right through the gates onto East Executive Avenue, a landscaped lane flanking the White House. Walk your bike—there is always a crowd of people lining up for tours of the White House. Here an elaborate security system has been disguised to maintain the aesthetics of the grounds.

Passing through the gateway at the other end, turn left on the sidewalk to arrive at 1600 Pennsylvania Avenue N.W., the address of every American president since John Adams. Designed by Irish-born architect James Hoban, the White House was painted its alabaster hue to cover damage caused by the British burning of 1814. Pennsylvania Avenue fronting the White House was closed to vehicular traffic in 1995. Drivers grumbled at the time, but walkers, joggers, in-line skaters, and cyclists have since turned this most famous stretch of street into a festive, car-free promenade.

Just past the White House on the right stands Blair-Lee House, a kind of guest house for the White House. You can usually tell who is visiting by the color of the flags flying. Next door is the Renwick Gallery, a Smithsonian museum devoted to objects made by artisans.

Carefully picking your way through one of Washington's busiest intersections, turn left on Seventeenth Street. Pass another fine art museum, the Corcoran Gallery, and the Organization of American States Building. Continue south to reach Constitution Avenue, a grand esplanade built on top of the old city canal. The last vestige of the canal, which was an open sewer as much as a waterway, is the old lockkeeper's house at Seventeenth and Constitution. Cross the road to find a winding path to the right to Constitution Gardens, a fifty-acre park dedicated in 1976. It features 5,000 trees, including honey locust, dogwood, and maple, and a 7½-acre lake that is home to carp, turtles, mallards, and geese.

Follow signs to the Vietnam Veterans Memorial. Designed by twenty-one-year-old architecture student Maya Lin, who won an open competition, the memorial features the names of 58,000 soldiers inscribed on a wall of polished black granite. Expect crowds, flowers, tears. Signs forbid you to bring your bike right up to "The Wall." Proceed up Henry Bacon Drive back to the Lincoln Memorial and double back to the Thompson Boat Center.

Rock Creek Park: D.C.

Distance:	9-mile loop
Approximate pedaling time:	1 hour
Terrain:	Rolling
Surface:	Paved multi-use trail, narrow at times
Things to see:	Oak Hill Cemetery, National Zoo, working grist mill
Facilities:	Rest rooms at Pierce Mill

In 1863 the naturalist John Burroughs wrote, "There is perhaps not another city in the Union that has on its threshold so much natural beauty and grandeur, such as men seek for in remote forests and mountains. A few touches of art would convert this whole region into a park unequalled in the world." The area he referred to was north of settled Washington, a forested place full of glens and meadows and ferns.

A few years later, the U.S. Army Corps of Engineers surveyed the same area, seeking a healthful new site for the White House. Instead they recommended that Rock Creek would make an excellent city greensward. Finally, in 1890, Burroughs's wish came true when Congress created 1,800-acre Rock Creek Park in the Northwest quadrant.

Today this stream valley once inhabited by the Algonquins provides recreation for many of D.C.'s 620,000 residents. In addition to boulder-strewn Rock Creek, it contains several other streams, tennis courts, hiking and bridle trails, a nature center, and historic buildings. The park provides an excellent commuting route for bikers from the neighborhoods of Cleveland Park, Woodley Park, Mount Pleasant, and Adams-Morgan to downtown D.C.

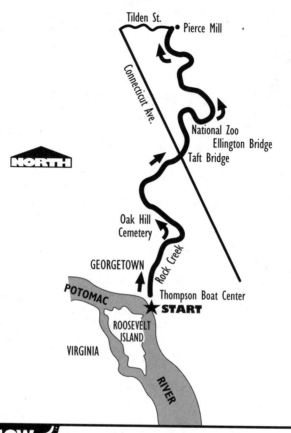

Tilden St. • Pierce Mill

Connecticut Ave.

National Zoo
Ellington Bridge
Taft Bridge

NORTH

Oak Hill
Cemetery

Rock Creek

GEORGETOWN

Thompson Boat Center
★ START

POTOMAC

ROOSEVELT
ISLAND

VIRGINIA

RIVER

HOW
to get
there
From north, Rock Creek Parkway south to Thompson's parking lot; turn right. From Mall, Virginia Avenue west across Rock Creek Parkway to Thompson's parking lot. From Virginia, Theodore Roosevelt Bridge or Memorial Bridge to Rock Creek Parkway to Thompson's parking lot. By Metro, Blue or Orange Line to Foggy Bottom/GWU station, about 1 mile walk or ride. From Metro station, walk south on Twenty-third Street (away from Washington Circle). Turn right on H Street, left on New Hampshire Avenue, and right on Virginia Avenue. Cross Rock Creek Parkway at crosswalk to reach parking lot of Thompson Boat Center. Follow one-lane road over short bridge to waterfront.

DIREC-TIONS for the ride

- From Thompson's Boat Center cross one-lane short bridge to parking lot.
- From parking lot, take curb cut at left to join Rock Creek trail.
- After passing exercise course, dismount and cross Rock Creek Parkway at crosswalk.
- Bear right at fork in trail and ride under arches of Ellington Bridge.
- At tunnel, turn left and ride through gate to path bordering Rock Creek.
- At service road crossing, turn left to ride over stone bridge into National Zoo.
- Return to trail via stone bridge. Turn left to head north.
- At parking lot near waterfall, turn left to visit Pierce Mill and Art Barn.
- Return to trail to join rides described in ride 4 or ride 10.
- To return to Thompson's Boat Center, turn around and retrace steps.

The park also provides a sanctuary for more wildlife than one might expect in the heart of a city. Look for mallards, wood ducks, and even a family of black-crowned night herons in the creek. You may also spot raccoons, foxes, deer, and beaver here.

A tour of Rock Creek Park begins at the creek's mouth on the Potomac. You can rent a bike (or a canoe or rowing shell) at the Harry T. Thompson Boat Center just off Virginia Avenue and Rock Creek Parkway N.W. Thompson's also has bike racks, lockers, water fountains, and rest rooms.

Leaving Thompson's, with the Watergate apartment complex and Kennedy Center on your right, turn left on the path heading north. Note on the right, on the other side of the Rock Creek Parkway and beneath a freeway ramp, the ruins of the Godey lime kiln, a vestige of a prosperous nineteenth-century industry. The path winds along the Parkway for the next 3 miles, at times almost grazing the road and then disappearing into thickets of woods. It crosses Rock Creek five times on bridges.

An exercise course parallels the route. On a spring day, the path becomes an olio of humanity, with Lycra-clad runners and cyclists mingling with baby strollers, birders, and groups of Chinese from the nearby embassy of the People's Republic. You'll even see children fishing and wading in the creek. In spring the embankment blazes with thousands of jonquils, daffodils, and tulips, while the woods bloom with dogwoods and redbud. In addition to the bright shades of crimson and yellow provided by these flora, the park always seems cool, green, and mossy thanks to its many trees and rock formations. The boulders that turn Rock Creek into cascades and provide dramatic outcroppings in the valley are the same type of Potomac Bluestone carved into building stone for the visitor center and handsomely crafted retaining walls within the park.

Passing under the decks of several old auto bridges, you pedal next to Oak Hill Cemetery, a twelve-acre burial ground founded in 1849 and filled with ornate Victorian monuments. As you pass under the Dumbarton Bridge, note the Indian heads carved in sandstone. This is also near the site of Lyons Mill, which was built in 1780 but collapsed with a roar in 1913. The stone piers for the bike-path bridge are all that remain of what was once Rock Creek's biggest industry.

After carefully crossing three parkway entrance ramps, you will thread under the Taft Bridge (1909) and then the Ellington Bridge (1935), named for jazz musician Duke Ellington and identifiable by three graceful arches rising 150 feet from the creek basin. Bear right on the path to travel under one of those arches. After crossing a small bridge with a narrow sidewalk, come to a parkway tunnel that contains an even slenderer path. Avoid the tunnel by turning left onto a smooth path parallel to Rock Creek. Glide over a stone bridge to the left to arrive at the National Zoological Park.

Founded in 1890 and laid out by Frederick Law Olmsted, the first landscape architect in the United States and designer of Central Park in New York City, the 163-acre zoo features hundreds of species of reptiles and mammals, including a giant panda and golden tamarind monkeys. Bicycle riding is not allowed in the zoo, but you can park your bike (locked securely!) or walk it to any of the nearby exhibits.. Lately, the zoo has been developing what it calls "BioParks," which are realistic and edifying replicas of diverse ecosystems. In 1992 the zoo realized this concept by building Amazonia, a $12 million rain-forest exhibition under a climate-controlled dome.

Back on the trail, you wind along through hardwood forest and dense alder bushes for a mile or so (be sure to check the creek for wood ducks and kingfishers) until arriving at Pierce Mill, the last of eight water-powered mills once driven by Rock Creek.

Built about 1820 from blue granite, the mill was restored in 1985 by the National Park Service. You can buy buckwheat and cornmeal, ground on site through a remarkable system of millstones, wooden gears, shafts, hoppers, and chutes. Close by are picnic grounds, rest rooms, and the Art Barn, a gallery installed in a former carriage house.

Continue north to the Pierce Mill parking lot. On weekends and holidays, this is the starting place for an exhilarating 12-mile ride up Beach Drive, closed to traffic. But on weekdays, the road reverts to a major commuter byway, and though it is marked an on-road bike path, I don't recommend it. If you're making this tour on a weekday, return to Thompson's the way you came. The remainder of Rock Creek Park is a treat best saved for weekends. To add about 8 miles, combine this ride with ride 11 (Upper Reaches of Rock Creek Park).

On the trip back, the first bridge you traverse is a concrete span stamped 1982. Look to the left across the road to view a bench carved from granite and inscribed JUSSERAND—PERSONAL TRIBUTE OF ESTEEM AND AFFECTION—1855–1932. (Jusserand was a French ambassador and friend of Teddy Roosevelt.)

Rock Creek Park
D.C. to Maryland and Back

Distance:	27-mile loop
Approximate pedaling time:	2–3 hours
Terrain:	Rolling
Surface:	Smooth roads closed to cars weekends and holidays, on-road routes, and paved off-road paths
Things to see:	Ravines of upper Rock Creek, Walter Reed Annex, Mormon Temple and gardens, Kensington antique center, Woodend estate, Miller cabin, Pierce Mill
Facilities:	Rest rooms at Pierce Mill and at Park Service Substation, food and antique shops in Kensington, gift shop at Woodend
Options:	1-mile side trip to Walter Reed Annex; 2.2-mile trip to historic Kensington

In the 1970s the National Park Service agreed to a bold experiment. On weekends and holidays, Beach Drive, one of the busiest roads leading into Rock Creek Park, would be closed to motorized traffic.

Perhaps to the pleasant surprise of the men in green, park use actually increased on auto-free days. So the Park Service institutionalized 7:00 A.M. to 7:00 P.M. closings of portions of the road. Meanwhile, an off-road trail was paved through the 2,700-acre Maryland section of Rock Creek Regional Park, providing an uninterrupted 12.5-mile ride from Pierce Mill in D.C. to Viers Mill in Maryland. (The trail was recently extended 5 miles farther north to Lake Needwood.)

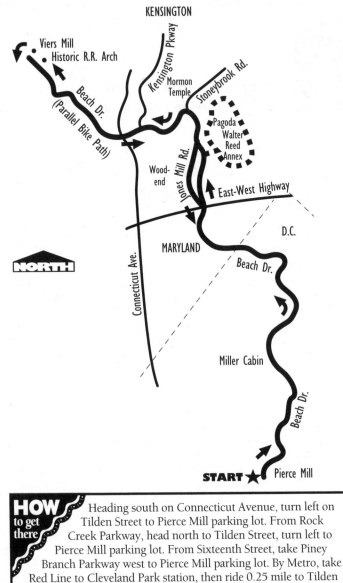

KENSINGTON

Viers Mill
Historic R.R. Arch

Beach Dr.
(Parallel Bike Path)

Kensington Pkway

Mormon
Temple

Stoneybrook Rd.

Pagoda
Walter
Reed
Annex

Wood-
end

Jones Mill Rd.

East-West Highway

D.C.

NORTH

MARYLAND

Connecticut Ave.

Beach Dr.

Miller Cabin

Beach Dr.

START ★ Pierce Mill

HOW to get there Heading south on Connecticut Avenue, turn left on Tilden Street to Pierce Mill parking lot. From Rock Creek Parkway, head north to Tilden Street, turn left to Pierce Mill parking lot. From Sixteenth Street, take Piney Branch Parkway west to Pierce Mill parking lot. By Metro, take Red Line to Cleveland Park station, then ride 0.25 mile to Tilden Street; turn right to Pierce Mill parking lot.

**DIREC-
TIONS**
for the ride

- From Pierce Mill parking area, head north on path, with creek to your right.
- Pass through auto barriers (weekends only) to enter Beach Drive.
- Stay on Beach Drive north past D.C. line. After passing playground and stables at right, turn right on East-West Highway.
- Cross East-West Highway at traffic light to pick up off-road trail.
- Pass small playground; then take optional right turn up zigzag path to Walter Reed Annex.
- Stay on path to Kensington Parkway (four-way stop). Turn right for detour to downtown Kensington.
- Return to path and turn right. Continue to Viers Mill and turn around. (Option: Continue 5 miles north to Lake Needwood.)
- To return on road, turn left onto Beach Drive.
- Pass Mormon Temple; then right on Jones Mill Road.
- Watch for Woodend sign; right on steep drive to explore estate.
- Return to Jones Mill, which turns into Beach Drive after the East-West Highway intersection.
- Beach Drive back to Pierce Mill.

This route is organized as a round-trip combining pathway and roadway travel. If you are nervous about cars, stick to the paths, but expect competition from strollers and pets.

The northern D.C. section of Rock Creek is flat-out gorgeous. Riding along a two-lane parkway designed to provide great vistas of hardwood forests and rushing waters, you can easily imagine yourself a hundred miles from the city.

After crossing into Maryland, pick up an off-road trail that leads you under the remains of an old Baltimore & Ohio train trestle and through wetlands and stands of evergreens. After passing a small playground, turn right to detour up an old footpath to the Walter Reed Army Medical Center Annex, a fascinating and eccentric campus on a high hill.

Built as a women's seminary nearly a century ago and annexed by the army during World War II, the 190-acre complex is almost like a pop-up sampler of world architecture. There's a Japanese pagoda, a Dutch windmill, a 600-year-old Roman fountain, a Bavarian resort hotel with stained-glass windows, and dormitory buildings that wouldn't look out of place in seventeenth-century Brussels. The idea was to provide the female seminarians with the sophistication afforded by world travel without exposing them to worldly evils. Unfortunately, the army says the badly deteriorating buildings will be torn down. Although preservationists promise a spirited fight, I wouldn't wait too long to see this architectural oddity. (For more information, contact Save Our Seminary Committee, P.O. Box 8274, Silver Spring, MD 20907.)

The next point of interest, accessible from Stonybrook Road, is the Washington Temple for the Church of Jesus Christ of the Latter-Day Saints. Soaring upright from a field of electric-green grass, the temple's profile from afar has been compared to Dorothy's first sighting of Oz. One of forty-one Mormon temples worldwide reserved for sacred ceremonies such as marriages and baptisms, the gleaming structure of white Alabama marble was completed in 1974. It rises 288 feet to a gold-plated statue of the angel Moroni, a Mormon prophet who lived around A.D. 400. The temple is closed to non-Mormons, but you can see photos of the sanctum sanctorum in the visitors center. The fifty-six-acre grounds are also worth a look.

Back on the trail, head west parallel to the creek through residential neighborhoods. At a four-way stop take a right on Kensington Parkway to visit the town of Kensington, a Victorian streetcar suburb with grand old frame houses and many antique shops. After taking tea at the Country Cupboard Tea Room (3750 Howard Avenue), return to the path to head north to Viers Mill, a county park.

Ride back to D.C. on Jones Mill Road and Beach Drive for different scenery and sights. This route affords a chance to see Woodend, the headquarters of the Audubon Naturalist Society of the Central Atlantic States. The forty-acre estate is cultivated to provide a variety of habitats that have attracted rabbits, bullfrogs, woodpeckers, and even wild turkey to the midst of this suburban area. There's also a formal garden and a Georgian mansion, which contains a shop selling books, calendars, binoculars, toys, and bird feeders. I find this shop particularly useful before Christmas. While the rest of Washington fumes in shopping traffic, I'm playing Santa with spokes, pedaling off to Woodend to stuff my panniers with gifts. Look closely for Woodend's small sign—it's easy to miss.

Back on a narrow, winding road lined with bungalows, you soon cross an intersection bisected by an old railroad right-of-way. This disused freight line is part of what local hikers and bikers hope will become the 11-mile Capital Crescent Trail linking Silver Spring, Maryland, with Georgetown and the C & O Canal National Historical Park. The stretch from Georgetown to downtown Bethesda is complete. It's at the heart of this book's next ride, "Capital Crescent Loop."

The return to Pierce Mill via Beach Drive is almost all downhill. Keep an eye out for crow-sized pileated woodpeckers attacking the hardwood trees lining this winding road. Also take a look at the former home of Joaquin Miller, the "Poet of the Sierras" who lived in Washington in the 1880s. Located on the west side of Beach Drive, it is reputed to be the only log cabin in D.C. The Miller Cabin hosts poetry readings on many summer nights.

Capital Crescent Loop

Distance:	14 miles
Approximate pedaling time:	2 hours
Terrain:	Flat
Surface:	Paved off-road recreational trails and suburban roads
Things to see:	Area's newest rail-to-trail conversion project, the C & O Canal, a bit of downtown Bethesda, old Chevy Chase houses, Rock Creek Park

Over the past decade or so, hundreds of communities across the country have turned abandoned railroad rights-of-way into attractive multi-use trails and linear parks. These "rail-to-trail" conversions have proved hugely popular. Their gentle grade makes them ideal for walking, jogging, in-line skating, cycling, and more.

At last count there were more than 700 completed rail-trails, totaling over 7,000 miles, in 46 U.S. states. They range in length from a couple of miles to a couple of hundred miles.

The Washington area joined the movement in a big way in the 1980s with the completion of the 45-mile long W & OD Trail from Arlington to the town of Purcellville, in the shadow the Blue Ridge mountains (see this book's next ride for complete details). Then came the 12-mile WB & A Trail in Prince George's and Anne Arundel counties.

Now, with the completion of its initial 7-mile stretch from the heart of Georgetown to downtown Bethesda, the Capital Crescent Trail joins the list. Although relatively short, it boasts Potomac River views, a restored trestle bridge over the C & O Canal, and a brick-vaulted railroad tunnel. It also offers a completely car-free commuting

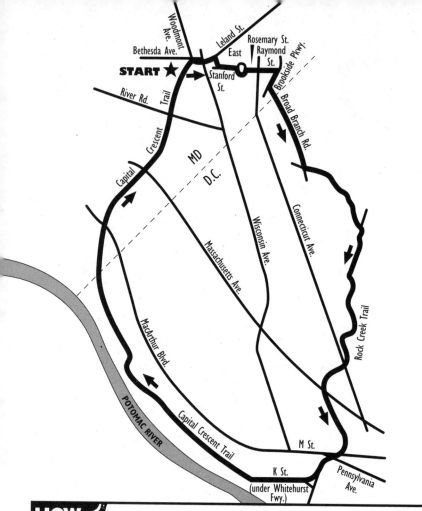

Woodmont Ave.

Leland St.

Rosemary St.
Raymond St.

Bethesda Ave.

East

Brookside Pkwy.

START ★

Stanford St.

River Rd.

Crescent Trail

Broad Branch Rd.

Capital

MD

D.C.

Wisconsin Ave.

Connecticut Ave.

Massachusetts Ave.

Rock Creek Trail

MacArthur Blvd.

Capital Crescent Trail

POTOMAC RIVER

M St.

Pennsylvania Ave.

K St.
(under Whitehurst Fwy.)

HOW to get there   Start at the Public parking lot at the corner of Bethesda and Woodmont avenues in Bethesda. From downtown D.C., follow Wisconsin Avenue to Bethesda, then turn left on Leland Street to Woodmont and Bethesda avenues. From the direction of Rockville, follow Wisconsin Avenue into town, then turn right onto Woodmont just past the National Institutes of Health and continue to Bethesda Avenue. Or, take the Metro to the Bethesda station on the Red Line. Exit via the Metro elevator onto Wisconsin Avenue, follow Wisconsin Avenue south for three blocks to Bethesda Avenue, then turn right for two blocks to Woodmont.

- From the entrance to the Capital Crescent Trail on Bethesda Avenue, turn right onto Woodmont Avenue. Woodmont merges with Leland Street just before Wisconsin Avenue.
- Cross Wisconsin Avenue, continuing straight on Leland Street.
- In three blocks, where Leland Street curves downhill to the left, continue straight onto East Street, then follow it to the right.
- Left onto Stanford Street to the traffic circle.
- Turn right onto Rosemary Street from the traffic circle.
- Cross Connecticut Avenue at the traffic light, continuing straight onto Raymond Street.
- Turn right onto Broad Branch Road, which crosses from Maryland into the District. Follow Broad Branch past Lafayette Elementary School.
- Broad Branch becomes a one-way road going the wrong way (against you) for one block before it crosses Military Road. Take to the sidewalk for this short stretch.
- Follow Broad Branch as it turns left two blocks after crossing Military. Be careful not to continue straight onto Linnean Street here.
- Continue on Broad Branch as it winds downhill into Rock Creek Park.
- Turn right into the small parking lot just before Broad Branch crosses Rock Creek and ends at Beach Drive.
- Continue onto the bike path at the end of this small parking area.
- Continue past Pierce Mill and across Tilden Street.
- Follow the Rock Creek bike path toward Georgetown. (See Ride 3 for details.)
- Pass under M Street and Pennsylvania Avenue overpasses.
- One hundred yards after riding beneath overpasses, turn right in path. This turnoff connects with K Street beneath the Whitehurst Freeway. You've missed it if you reach Thompson's Boat House in another hundred yards.
- Ride the full length of K Street beneath the Whitehurst Freeway.

- Continue straight onto the Capital Crescent Trail at the very end of K Street.
- Follow the Capital Crescent Trail for its entire length back to Bethesda. Along the way, you'll ride alongside the C&O Canal before crossing a bridge over it; pass through a tunnel beneath MacArthur Boulevard; cross a bridge over Massachusetts Avenue; dismount to cross busy River Road; and cross Little Falls Parkway.
- Reach the Trail's end at Bethesda Avenue.

---

route from Bethesda to downtown. And for longer rides it features direct connections to the C & O towpath (Ride 14), Rock Creek Park (Rides 3 and 4), and Virginia's extensive trail system (Rides 1, 15, and 16).

This ride connects the Capital Crescent Trail, an on-road stretch through Chevy Chase, and Rock Creek Park. The resulting loop is high on fun, short on cars, and completely lacking in noticeable hills.

Start in downtown Bethesda, at the corner of Woodmont and Bethesda avenues. Look for the entrance to the Capital Crescent Trail between the public parking lot on the corner and the car dealership on Bethesda Avenue. A doughnut shop, two bagel stores, and a gourmet coffee shop—all within yards of the trailhead—offer an opportunity to fuel up for your ride. In the spirit of saving the best for last, though, ride away from the trail, following Woodmont Avenue and Leland Street across Wisconsin Avenue and into the suburban village of Chevy Chase.

This is one of Washington's classic old neighborhoods. You'll pass older bungalows and colonial-style homes along East, Stanford, and Rosemary streets. Grand Victorians and Federal-style homes line the route on the other side of Connecticut Avenue.

Follow Broad Branch Road into the District itself. The road shoots downhill through a nice residential neighborhood, then corkscrews through a ravine into Rock Creek Park. Turn right into the small parking lot just before Broad Branch Road crosses a short bridge over Rock Creek itself. Hop onto the bike path here, passing by Pierce

Mill, and head downtown toward the National Zoo and Georgetown (see Ride 3 for complete details on this stretch).

Now comes the only tricky part. About a hundred yards after crossing beneath the M Street and Pennsylvania Avenue overpasses, turn right as a fork of the bike path veers off to connect with K Street beneath the Whitehurst Freeway. (You've gone too far if you reach Thompson's Boat House on the right in another hundred yards.) Ride the length of K street, passing the Washington Harbor development and the rest of Georgetown's waterfront on the left. At the very end, where K Street ends, the Capital Crescent Trail begins.

This brand-new trail (first paved in 1995), traces the east bank of the Potomac River for a few miles before turning inland toward Bethesda. The views are best in fall or early spring, before thick growth turns it into a tunnel of greenery. You'll ride alongside the C & O Canal towpath for a short stretch. The trail then curves right, crossing a restored railroad trestle bridge over the canal. Be sure to rest here for the view.

The trail's approximate midway point is marked by a cavernous, brick-vaulted tunnel beneath MacArthur Boulevard. Keep riding until you reach River Road, the trail's first obstacle since Georgetown. Montgomery County plans to build a bridge to carry the trail over this busy four-lane road. Until that happens, though, dismount and cross carefully. From here, there are two additional but less challenging street crossings. The Bethesda public swimming pool at Little Falls Road will seem particularly welcoming on a hot summer day. (Be sure to pack a bathing suit, towel, and about $10 per person for snacks and entrance fees.) From there, it's just another half-mile to the trail's end at Bethesda and Woodmont avenues.

The W & OD Trail
through Virginia Countryside

Distance:	39 miles, one way
Approximate pedaling time:	4 hours
Terrain:	Mostly flat and straight
Surface:	Paved multi-use trail
Things to see:	Historic train stations, farms, creeks, downtown Leesburg historic district
Facilities:	Rest rooms, restaurants, bike shops, country store

The Washington and Old Dominion Railroad never was very successful. Founded in 1847 to connect towns on the Potomac to resort towns in the Blue Ridge Mountains, the rail line locals dubbed the "Virginia Creeper" ran sporadically and lost money for more than a century until closing for good in 1968.

Today, however, the W & OD line is a stunning success. Its 100-foot-wide right-of-way has been converted to a park stretching from the Arlington/Alexandria border to the rural town of Purcellville, 45 miles away. The Northern Virginia Regional Park Authority has created one of the most convenient, safe, and interesting trails in the capital region. You can easily reach the W & OD by Metrorail, super-highway, or other off-road trails. From Vienna to Purcellville, the wide, paved trail is augmented by a separate 30-mile gravel bridle path. The Park Authority constructed or restored seventeen bridges to whisk cyclists over stream beds and busy roads.

Dozens of roads and parking lots connect to the W & OD, so you can pick a starting point at will. One of the most popular is the Metrorail station in East Falls Church, from where you will encounter only a few miles of suburbia before getting to the "good

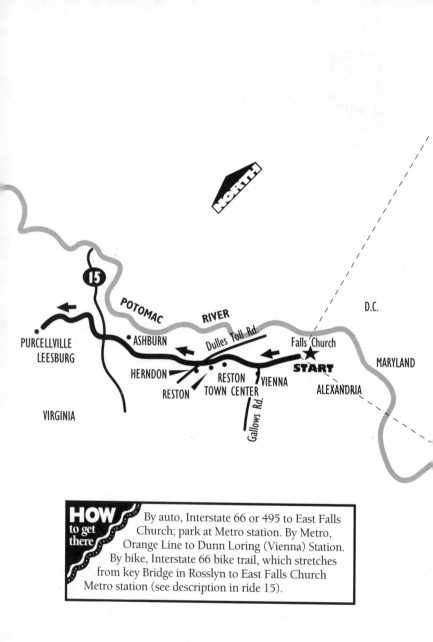

NORTH

15

POTOMAC RIVER

PURCELLVILLE
LEESBURG

ASHBURN

Dulles Toll Rd.

Falls Church

D.C.

MARYLAND

START

HERNDON

RESTON TOWN CENTER

VIENNA

RESTON

ALEXANDRIA

Gallows Rd.

VIRGINIA

HOW to get there By auto, Interstate 66 or 495 to East Falls Church; park at Metro station. By Metro, Orange Line to Dunn Loring (Vienna) Station. By bike, Interstate 66 bike trail, which stretches from key Bridge in Rosslyn to East Falls Church Metro station (see description in ride 15).

DIREC-TIONS for the ride

- From Dunn Loring (Vienna) Metrorail station, turn left onto Gallows Road. Ride on sidewalk if traffic is heavy.
- Turn left on W & OD trail to head toward Purcellville. Trail is well marked.
- Turn right on W & OD trail to head toward Arlington. Trail is well marked.

stuff." Falls Church and Vienna, the next town along the trail, have interesting historic areas. In particular, the old train depot in Vienna now houses an elaborate model train operated by the Northern Virginia Model Railroaders Association. Traversing these towns does require some tedious crossings of busy roads and shopping plazas.

For a shorter ride that skips this suburban stretch, begin near the 17-mile marker in the planned community of Reston. Reston was founded in 1963 by Robert E. Simon, who envisioned a utopian community of mixed ages and income levels. Until recently, most of Reston looked like typical suburbia, but the new Reston Town Center has brought some urban splash. Located smack-up against the W & OD, the eighty-five-acre area tries to re-create an open-air, lively city neighborhood: brick sidewalks, outdoor cafes, sixty shops of the BenneGapLimited variety, movie theaters, linden trees lined up along the streets, and a European-style central fountain. In keeping with the haute boutique atmosphere, there's a fancy bike shop that features a granite waterfall, polished hardwood floors—and bike rentals. A few miles ahead, the old burgs of Herndon and Sterling have retained their neat town centers. Farther west, the cyclist encounters open fields and picturesque streams, beginning with Broad Run.

The scenery is now divided between broad vistas and low gullies lined by thick underbrush. More than 450 wildflower species grow along the W & OD, including Virginia Creeper, a vine with berries and five-pronged leaves. After passing an old quarry, you come to the country town of Ashburn. Be sure to stop at Partlow's Store, where

45

you can buy anything from bananas to wading boots. The friendly dog on the porch *will* try to steal your granola bars.

Ride over an old railroad bridge over Goose Creek, and soon you're on the outskirts of Leesburg, seat of Loudoun County. Turn right on Catoctin Circle and right again on Market Street for a look at the old courthouse and the narrow streets of the historic district. The town was first named Georgetown after the king, and renamed in the 1700s for Thomas Lee, a wily planter and trader who excelled at Indian negotiations.

Leesburg was a Civil War site of minor importance. In an effort to dislodge Confederate troops in 1861, Union forces invaded the town via the 100-foot cliffs of Ball's Bluff. They were spectacularly rebuffed and suffered 1,700 casualties. An apocryphal tale has it that corpses of the blue brigade washed up 40 miles downriver in Washington's commercial district.

The W & OD runs another 9 miles west through rolling Loudoun County, ending in the old town of Purcellville. If the Park Authority reaches its goal of extending the trail a few miles more to Bluemont, they will have effected a connection to the 2,100-mile Appalachian Trail for hiking. In 1987 the U.S. Department of the Interior designated the whole park as a National Recreation Trail.

If you're interested in exploring the W & OD thoroughly, look for the fifty-six page *W & OD Trail Guide* at local bike shops or Northern Virginia Regional Parks offices. Or call the W & OD Trail office at (703) 729–0596 to order a copy.

Mount Vernon Trail
to Old Town Alexandria

Distance:	26-mile loop
Approximate pedaling time:	2–3 hours
Terrain:	Flat
Surface:	Smooth off-road trails and some busy roads
Things to see:	Jefferson Memorial, National Airport, sailing marina, historic Alexandria, Hunting Creek wildlife area
Facilities:	Rest rooms, snack bar, and bike shop at Daingerfield Island Marina, Georgetown section of C & O Canal

On Sunday mornings, I often slip away to points usually too crowded to enjoy intimately. My avenue for this furtive endeavor is the Mount Vernon Trail, an 18.5-mile off-road path that links Washington with the estate of the president for whom the city was named. In between lies historic Alexandria, Virginia, a minor port in colonial America and a major tourist attraction today. The trip back includes the even older settlement of Georgetown.

The trail parallels the George Washington Memorial Parkway, a scenic road built in 1932 for the bicentennial of the first president's birth. This ride begins at Harry T. Thompson Boat Center in Washington. (Turn to the end of this chapter for an alternative starting point at Theodore Roosevelt Island on the Virginia side.) Leaving Thompson's, turn right onto a path. As described in Ride 1, proceed to the Jefferson Memorial and cross the Fourteenth Street Bridge bike path to Virginia. At the end of the bridge, bear right onto a short stretch of path that drops down to river level. Turn right onto the Mount Vernon trail, heading downriver.

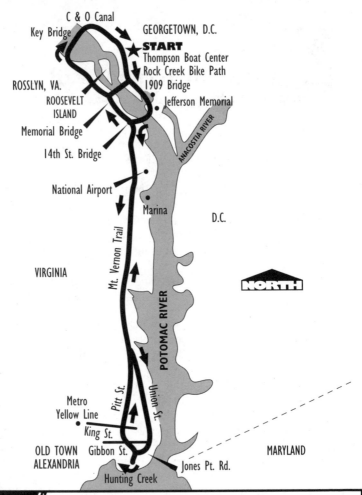

C & O Canal
Key Bridge
GEORGETOWN, D.C.
★ **START**
Thompson Boat Center
Rock Creek Bike Path
1909 Bridge
ROSSLYN, VA.
ROOSEVELT ISLAND
Jefferson Memorial
Memorial Bridge
14th St. Bridge
National Airport
Marina
D.C.
VIRGINIA
NORTH
Mt. Vernon Trail
POTOMAC RIVER
Metro
Yellow Line
Pitt St.
Union St.
King St.
OLD TOWN
ALEXANDRIA
Gibbon St.
Jones Pt. Rd.
MARYLAND
Hunting Creek

HOW to get there From north, Rock Creek Parkway to Thompson's parking lot; turn right. From the Mall, Virginia Avenue west across Rock Creek Parkway to Thompson's parking lot. From Virginia, Roosevelt Bridge or Memorial Bridge to Rock Creek Parkway to Thompson's. By Metro, Blue or Orange Line to Foggy Bottom/GWU, about a 1-mile walk or ride. From Metro station, walk south on Twenty-third Street (away from Washington Circle). Turn right on H Street, left on New Hampshire Avenue, and right on Virginia Avenue. Cross Rock Creek Parkway at crosswalk to reach parking lot of Thompson Boat Center. Follow one-lane road over short bridge to waterfront.

- From Thompson Boat Center, right on bike path toward Watergate apartments and Kennedy Center, Potomac River on right.
- Cross parkway intersection to reach path continuing through volleyball courts.
- Ride or walk through two short bridge underpasses.
- Straight through traffic circle at Ericsson Monument to Ohio Drive.
- Straight on Ohio Drive past soccer fields to cross 1909 bridge. Left at circular garden.
- Across from Jefferson Memorial entrance, right at curb cut to reach bikeway over Fourteenth Street Bridge.
- Cross bridge and bear right on bike path down to river level. Turn right onto Mount Vernon Trail, heading downriver.
- Follow trail signs past National Airport and sailing marina.
- In 4 miles, cross railroad tracks. Trail continues on North Union Street in Old Town Alexandria.
- At Gibbon Street, bear left on off-road bike path. Path rejoins Jones Point Road parallel to Interstate 95.
- Follow on-road path to Hunting Towers apartment complex at Washington Street. Left on sidewalk.
- Turn around at Hunting Creek bridge. Retrace steps; bear left on Royal Street, on-road bike route through upper Old Town.
- Right on Queen Street. Left on Union to rejoin Mount Vernon route.
- Straight on Mount Vernon Path north to Key Bridge, which crosses the river to Georgetown.
- Right to cross bridge; right on M Street. Right on Thirty-fourth Street.
- Foot ramp to C & O Canal.
- Left to reach trailhead of C & O Canal.
- Right on bike path at Rock Creek.
- Right to Thompson Boat Center.

Passing a soccer field on the right, come to Gravelly Point, a good place to see the monuments—and landing jets—in profile. Continue through a parking lot to traverse National Airport. This part isn't the most scenic ride in the world, but it's not without interest. Much of the 750-acre airport was built in the 1930s under WPA programs, and the original buildings retain some of their streamlined, New Deal charm. In 1994, work began on a mammoth new main terminal. Carefully cross four parkway ramps to reach the marina at Daingerfield Island. On any given day, this windswept spit attracts hundreds of sailors, sunbathers, and windsurfers. You will also find a snack bar, bike shop, tony restaurant, and rest rooms. Bike and boat rentals are available at the marina. For information call (703) 548–9027.

Now head south through a marsh full of cattails. Keep an eye out for circling hawks. When the path comes to a fork, bear left for a ride *above* the Potomac. To get around the area's industrial property, the Park Service built a cantilevered trail protruding from a retaining wall and supported by diagonal steel struts. The scenery is now a mixture of new office parks, an old rail line, Potomac vistas, and Alexandria's network of waterfront parks. After crossing the railroad bed, graded flush with the road, reach North Union Street, heading for Alexandria's historic heart.

Founded by Scottish immigrants and laid out in 1749 with help from surveyor George Washington, Alexandria grew into a thriving tobacco port. In 1791 the burg was incorporated into the nascent District of Columbia. Town leaders agitated successfully for a return to mother Virginia in 1846. Alexandria escaped destruction during the Civil War, thereby retaining a large collection of brick and gingerbread houses of all eras.

It's easy to roam the gridiron of 200 city blocks by bicycle. Particularly worthwhile are Queen and Prince streets (perpendicular to the river), and Royal and St. Aspaph streets (parallel to the waterfront). The city's housing trademark is the oblong "flounder house," whose side porch looks like it should face front. King Street hums with bookshops, pubs, and restaurants. Heading uphill, it leads to the 330-foot-tall George Washington Masonic Memorial, the area's second-tallest building after the Washington Monument.

Be sure to visit historic Christ Church, attended by both George Washington and Robert E. Lee; the Athenaeum, a history museum; and the Torpedo Factory, a World War I munitions plant that now houses 200 artists' studios. There's a visitors center at 221 King Street.

Back on your two-wheeler, head south on North Union Street. Follow bike-path signs until you reach busy Washington Street. The route continues on a sidewalk. In a few hundred feet stop at a stone bridge and pull out your lightweight binoculars. Among tidal flats and rotting piers, you can spot snowy egrets, hooded mergansers, and bufflehead ducks, not to mention eagles and falcons.

Rather than moving on to Mount Vernon—the route there from Alexandria is covered in the next chapter—turn around for a slightly different return to Washington. First detour to Jones Point, where an old whitewashed lighthouse marks the city's original southern tip. Then follow an alternate bike route to Royal Street, a typical Old Town lane with narrow row houses. Turn left on King Street to visit the Masonic Memorial or catch Metrorail's Yellow Line back to downtown D.C. Otherwise, head north to Princess Street, turn right, and rejoin the bike path at Founders Park on the waterfront.

In 4 miles, bypass the Fourteenth Street Bridge and keep straight. Pass the Lady Bird Johnson Park and bear right as the trail forks to follow it under Memorial Bridge. Pedal by eighty-eight-acre Theodore Roosevelt Island, once a country estate and now a park. Downshift to ascend a new highway overpass to high-rise Rosslyn, Virginia. Turn right to reach Key Bridge and its broad foot/bike path. The bridge affords spectacular views. Now in Georgetown, turn right on M Street and right again on Thirty-fourth Street to reach the C & O Canal, to be described in coming rides. The path turns from pack dirt to brick to end in a T at Rock Creek. Turn right to reach Thompson's parking area in about 150 feet.

To shorten this ride and skip its two crossings over the Potomac River, start at Theodore Roosevelt Island on the Virginia side. Park in the lot just off the George Washington Memorial Parkway. Ride south on the new boardwalk/asphalt path to connect with the Mount Vernon Trail. When you return, take the time to explore at least some of the island's 2.5 miles of trails and its memorial plaza.

Mount Vernon Trail
Alexandria to Mount Vernon

Distance:	18-mile loop
Approximate pedaling time:	2 hours
Terrain:	Rolling
Surface:	Smooth off-road trails and boardwalks
Things to see:	Old Town Alexandria, Dyke Marsh, Fort Hunt Park, Riverside Park, Mount Vernon
Facilities:	Rest rooms at parks, food and souvenirs at Mount Vernon
Option:	6-mile trip to Woodlawn Plantation

The final 8-mile leg of the Mount Vernon Trail resembles a trip to a country estate. It is far more bucolic than the first section. The terrain is also more undulating, which provides some Potomac views.

Start in Old Town Alexandria at the King Street Metrorail station. You can either arrive by Metro during valid hours for bike passes (see Appendix) or park at the station. Head away from the station on King Street, which is lined with antique stores and pubs. In 1 mile turn right on Union Street to join the Mount Vernon Trail.

As described in ride 7, follow signs to Hunting Creek, then continue straight, with a marshy area of the Potomac due left. You will soon arrive at two parks. The first, Belle Haven, indeed provides respite for sailors, picnickers, and bird-watchers. In season you can rent small sailboats here. Next door stands Dyke Marsh, a 240-acre wildlife preserve rescued from an earlier life as a gravel pit. If it's not muddy, ride out on a spit that juts into the Potomac for a look at this sprawling cattail marsh. In spring the sanctuary hosts 250 bird species, not to mention wild iris, muskrats, frogs, and turtles. It's a glimpse of what these banks looked like two centuries ago.

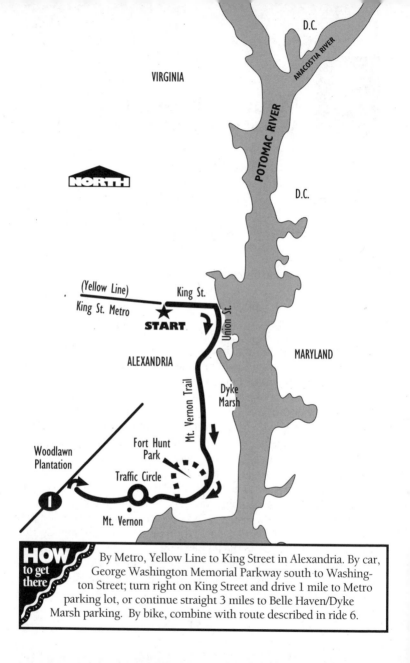

D.C.

ANACOSTIA RIVER

VIRGINIA

POTOMAC RIVER

NORTH

D.C.

(Yellow Line)
King St. Metro

King St.

Union St.

MARYLAND

★
START

ALEXANDRIA

Mt. Vernon Trail

Dyke
Marsh

Woodlawn
Plantation

Fort Hunt
Park

Traffic Circle

1

Mt. Vernon

HOW to get there   By Metro, Yellow Line to King Street in Alexandria. By car, George Washington Memorial Parkway south to Washington Street; turn right on King Street and drive 1 mile to Metro parking lot, or continue straight 3 miles to Belle Haven/Dyke Marsh parking. By bike, combine with route described in ride 6.

DIREC-TIONS for the ride

■ Start in Alexandria at King Street Metro or Belle Haven picnic area (the latter cuts about 3 miles from trip).

■ From King Street, ride north 1 mile to Union Street. Turn right.

■ Follow bike-path signs to Hunting Towers apartments on Washington Street. Bear left on sidewalk, which turns into bike path again shortly.

■ Follow bike-path signs to Mount Vernon, with optional side trips to Dyke Marsh (1-mile round-trip on dirt path) and Fort Hunt Park (1-mile loop on park road).

■ Retrace path back to starting point.

Option: At Mount Vernon, bear right at traffic circle and turn right on Mount Vernon Highway west. Off-road bike path is available, but on-road shoulder is fairly wide and flat. In 3 miles, carefully cross Route 1 to enter Woodlawn Plantation.

Back on the route to Mount Vernon, the trail continues on a boardwalk through the marsh. There's a bench for pausing and pondering. Last time there I was treated to a five-minute dogfight as a fish hawk, its talons flaring, buzzed any herons and hawks that dared enter its territory.

Soon the path becomes more winding as hardwood forest closes in. After crossing a bridge across the parkway—noting the handsome construction of the stone span—glide downhill on a grassy median planted with blooming trees and evergreens, then climb again up to a bluff with fine views. The stone structure across the river is Fort Washington, a star-shaped fortress designed by Washington planner Pierre L'Enfant. Coast down to Fort Hunt Park, which has its own military ruins among 156 acres of picnic grounds.

Other sites worth visiting along the path include River Farm, a former holding of George Washington that is now the headquarters of the American Horticultural Society (public welcome to tour gardens and picnic on the river) and Riverside Park, a picnic area on a mini-spit of land next to Little Hunting Creek, just before the approach to Mount Vernon.

The remainder of the trail stays close to inlets and bays of the river until it jinks to the right and then climbs, signaling the approach to the estate of George and Martha Washington. Located on high ground on a bend in the river, the crescent-shaped house is surprisingly small but faultlessly elegant. Its Georgian facade was designed to fool the eye. It resembles sandstone but, when tapped, resounds with a knock. To simulate more expensive material, the colonials molded wood into masonrylike blocks and mixed sand with the paint for a rough finish.

The grounds also feature winding paths, formal gardens, trees planted by the general himself, and outbuildings filled with colonial tools and carriages. The estate is lovingly maintained and interpreted by the Mount Vernon Ladies' Association, which also provides tours. In 1858 the group rescued Mount Vernon from ruin, thereby launching the American historic preservation movement—and making possible the survival of many other sites noted in this book.

Leaving Mount Vernon, carefully cross a traffic circle for an optional 6-mile round-trip to another site associated with Washington. The Mount Vernon Highway leads to Woodlawn Plantation, once home to Washington's adopted daughter, Nelly Custis Lewis. It's now a house museum run by the National Trust for Historic Preservation. Here the Garden Club of Virginia carefully tends thirty-six rose beds hedged by dwarf species of English boxwood. Also on the grounds is a Frank Lloyd Wright house, which the National Trust rescued from a highway's path and moved to Woodlawn in the 1950s.

Rosemont Ramble

Distance:	8 miles
Approximate pedaling time:	90 minutes
Terrain:	Flat with one climb
Surface:	Good suburban roads and on-road bike lanes
Things to see:	Torpedo Factory, shops of King Street, The Lyceum, Gentry Row, George Washington Masonic Memorial, neighborhoods of Rosemont and Del Ray
Facilities:	Shops, rest rooms, Metrorail stop

This is a sightseeing figure eight of Alexandria that shows off both eighteenth-century Old Town and late-nineteenth-century historic neighborhoods. It is easily reached by Metro or bike paths from D.C.

Start at the King Street Metrorail station about 1 mile west of the Potomac River. The main landmark is a big one: the 330-foot-tall, gray pyramidal tower of the George Washington Masonic Memorial, built earlier in this century with $5 million donated by three million members of the Masonic order. It's the region's tallest structure after the Washington Monument (and, like the big white needle, it's open to the public, with an elevator ride to the top). Pause en route to see things like the dioramas depicting Masonic deeds and the trowel G.W. used to lay the U.S. Capitol's cornerstone. Just south of the temple is Alexandria Union Station, much less grand than D.C.'s Union Station, but a quaint stop on Amtrak's southern route nonetheless.

Leave the Metro station and head north under the railroad tracks on King Street. Take your first right onto Russell Road. You are entering Rosemont, a pre–World War I suburb that the city of Alexandria

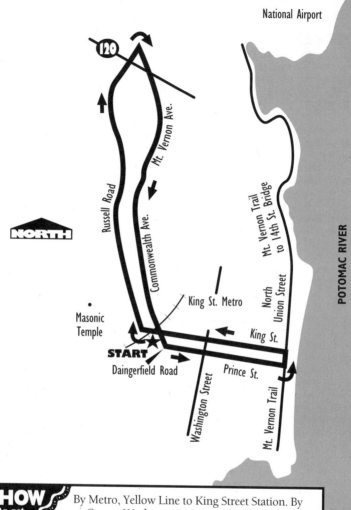

National Airport

120

Russell Road

Mt. Vernon Ave.

Commonwealth Ave.

NORTH

POTOMAC RIVER

Mt. Vernon Trail to 14th St. Bridge

North Union Street

King St. Metro

Masonic Temple

King St.

START

Daingerfield Road

Prince St.

Washington Street

Mt. Vernon Trail

HOW to get there — By Metro, Yellow Line to King Street Station. By car, George Washington Memorial Parkway south to Washington Street; turn right on King Street and drive 1 mile to Metro parking lot. By bike, take Mount Vernon Trail from north or south to King Street and ride 1 mile to Metro station.

DIREC-TIONS
for the ride

- From King Street Metro, go under tracks on King Street.
- Bear right at first intersection on Russell Road.
- Follow Russell for about 30 blocks until it ends at Y intersection.
- Hard right on Mount Vernon Avenue.
- At Y intersection, bear right on Commonwealth Avenue and follow for 25 blocks.
- Pass under railroad tracks and turn left at light onto Daingerfield Road.
- First left onto Prince Street.
- Straight on Prince Street about 1 mile to North Union.
- Left on North Union.
- After 1 block, left on King Street.
- Straight for 1 mile back to King Street Metro station.

annexed in 1915. Rosemont's raison d'être was the Washington, Alexandria, and Mt. Vernon electric streetcar line, which brought downtown D.C. within a nickel and eighteen minutes. (A 1909 ad promised free streetcar tickets to come view model homes priced from $750 to $1,200.) The streetcar faded away in the 1930s, but Rosemont continued to thrive and today is a well-preserved neighborhood with neat bungalows mixed in among grander houses with wraparound porches.

A marked bike lane along Russell Road whisks you through Rosemont before you start climbing the North Ridge. Stop at Alexandria Country Day school at the top of the hill on the left for an excellent view over the Potomac to Maryland. Also known as Shuter's Hill, the ridge was seized by Union troops during the Civil War and laid bare so lookouts would have clear sightlines.

Rosemont segues into Del Ray, a blue-collar neighborhood built to house railroad workers for nearby Potomac Yards. (Del Ray was formerly called Potomac, but its cottages would never be confused with the plummy manses across the river in Potomac, Maryland.) The

320-acre freight yards may soon give way to a massive new development called Potomac 2020. After heading downhill, double back through Rosemont along commercial Mount Vernon Avenue. Bear right onto bike-laned Commonwealth Avenue, where the trolley formerly ran on the median strip.

After again threading under the Metrorail tracks and turning left on Daingerfield Road, head east on Prince Street toward the river. The vacant traffic triangle you pass while making the turn is the former site of Hooff's Run, a creek now channeled through underground pipes.

Alexandria was intended to be a grand and great city until it was outstripped as a port, and its early architecture reflects it. Prince Street is one of Old Town's oldest and most intact thoroughfares. A series of rowhouses in the 200 block, Gentry Row, dates from 1752 to 1795; 200 Prince belonged to Robert Townshend Hooe, the city's first elected mayor. Another house belonged to Dr. James Craik, the physician at George Washington's side when he died; Craik's colleague and neighbor Dr. Elisha Cullen Dick cut the pendulum cords on the first president's clock to record the time of death. Across the street, the Greek Revival Lyceum, built as a library in 1839, has housed the city's history museum since 1985. At the corner of Prince and busy Washington streets stands a bronze statue of R. E. Lee Camp, confederate soldier. The monument offends some, but the Virginia legislature passed a special bill in 1890 ensuring it would never be moved.

Continue down Prince (the last block is cobblestone) to North Union and visit the artsy-craftsy Torpedo Factory (which has a new waterfront "food court," à la shopping malls) before returning to the start via King Street, Old Town's busiest and boutique-iest boulevard. The corner of King and Pitt recorded the Civil War's first casualty: A Union colonel named Ellsworth was shot dead after he tore a Confederate flag from a tavern.

Reservoir–Great Falls Run

Distance:	24-mile loop
Approximate pedaling time:	3 hours
Terrain:	Flat with two big hills
Surface:	Smooth roads, bike paths
Things to see:	Bluffs overlooking river, Glen Echo Park, Clara Barton House, Cabin John viaduct, Great Falls Tavern
Facilities:	Convenience food along route, health-food co-op, rest rooms at Glen Echo and Great Falls
Option:	Return trip through C & O Canal National Historical Park

This jaunt should be dedicated to Quartermaster General Montgomery C. Meigs, a Civil War hero and engineer who designed the 10-mile-long aqueduct system that still provides Washington with fresh water. In the process he created a refreshing route for modern-day cyclists. The Meigs legacy is announced by a series of whimsical structures that now line this popular cycling route to Great Falls National Park in Maryland.

Start at the confluence of Reservoir Road and MacArthur Boulevard, near a pumping structure that Meigs disguised as a classical temple. The reservoir's grounds are populated by black vultures, ducks, and even red fox. You are in the heart of the city's Palisades enclave, dense with trees and rambling old wood-frame houses. Head west on MacArthur Boulevard, the neighborhood's main street, past such landmarks as a one-room schoolhouse and the Art Deco MacArthur Theater. The road is winding and busy, but the shoulder is wide and traffic moves slowly.

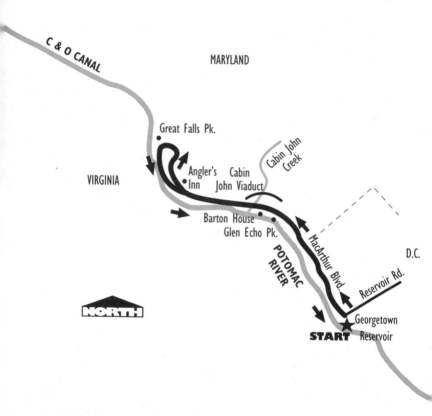

C & O CANAL

MARYLAND

Great Falls Pk.

Angler's Inn

Cabin John Viaduct

Cabin John Creek

VIRGINIA

Barton House
Glen Echo Pk.

POTOMAC RIVER

MacArthur Blvd

D.C.

Reservoir Rd.

NORTH

Georgetown Reservoir

START

HOW to get there From Georgetown, west on Canal Road to Arizona Avenue; turn right, and right again on MacArthur Boulevard to reach Reservoir Road intersection. From Virginia, cross Chain Bridge, right on Canal Road, left on Arizona, right on MacArthur. From Maryland, east on MacArthur to Reservoir intersection. Park in the neighborhood (note weekday restrictions on signs) or in shopping areas on MacArthur Boulevard.

DIREC-TIONS for the ride

- From MacArthur Boulevard and Reservoir Road, head west on shoulder of MacArthur. After passing Dalecarlia Reservoir, road narrows to two lanes. Cross MacArthur to off-road bike path that begins on left.
- Follow bike path to parking area for Glen Echo Park and Clara Barton National Historic Site, about 4 miles from ride start.
- Off-road path ends in another 5 miles. Follow on-road route as MacArthur Boulevard curves right past Old Angler's Inn for a long, winding climb trhough the woods.
- At crest of hill, turn left into Great Falls Park as Falls Road turns right. Swift descent on-road leads to visitors center.
- Retrace steps back to Washington. Or return via C & O Canal towpath, a route that requires carrying your bike over some rocks near Great Falls. In 12 miles, at Fletcher's Boat House, cross bridge over canal. Cross Canal Road to Reservoir Road. Ride up steep hill to intersection of Reservoir and MacArthur (see ride 13).

At the city line, marked by another reservoir, the boulevard narrows to a two-lane road. Switch to the bike path at left, parallel to oncoming traffic. Climb a short but steep hill to reach the Brookmont neighborhood, marked by Bonfield's service station, a fixture for more than six decades. With its pink-and-green neon sign and whitewashed siding, Bonfield's looks like a cross between an old farmhouse and an early fast-food restaurant. The owner will sell you a soda pop or rent inner tubes for a float down the Potomac.

Next, the path traces a precipice high above the river. This was the old trolley route (described by John Dos Passos in his *U.S.A.* trilogy) from downtown to the country. Ruins of the old trestle remain among the sycamore trees and thorny undergrowth. For nearly seventy years the transit line's terminus was Glen Echo amusement park. After the park closed in 1968, the National Park Service acquired the land to create a cultural center. The 1921 Dentzel carousel has been restored, calliope intact, and is open spring through fall. Also pre-

served are the bumper-car shed and the Spanish Ballroom, still used for swing dances and concerts. This may be the world's only Art Deco ghost town—well worth a look. Reach Glen Echo by turning left onto Oxford Road, just past a small traffic circle.

Before leaving the streamlined spires of Glen Echo, visit the neighboring Clara Barton National Historic Site, a turreted Victorian house where the saintly founder of the American Red Cross spent her last fifteen years. It's open every day except national holidays.

Continuing west alongside MacArthur Boulevard, the trail meanders through the old towns of Glen Echo and Cabin John. Slow down to cross a bridge wide enough for only one lane of cars and one lane of bicycles. This is Meigs's great 220-foot-long aqueduct, constructed to convey 10,000 gallons of water hourly over the valley of Cabin John Creek. It still does the job and carries rush-hour traffic in style as well.

Now look for a carved sign announcing the Wild Bird Center. The red bungalow will be under siege from hundreds of birds. This emporium for the avian-crazed sells everything from suet cakes to electronic birdbath warmers. The owner has installed at least a score of feeders out front, attracting sparrows, who eat the sunflower seeds, and hawks, who eat the sparrows. A bit up the road on the right, hearty (and organic) human food is available at the Bethesda Co-op. The Proteus bike shop is just down the block at 7945 MacArthur Boulevard, Cabin John, Maryland, (301) 229–5900.

The next landmark, on the left, is the U.S. Navy's Carderock Division of Naval Surface Warfare Center, which resembles a mile-long Quonset hut. The shed contains a tank for testing scale models of ships. Continue parallel to MacArthur Boulevard and its clusters of Victorian houses. These hills were once alive with gold mines, opened during the Civil War and abandoned since 1935.

By now cars will be whizzing by with splinter-shaped boats mounted on their roofs. These are kayakers heading for the mouth of Mather Gorge, whose rapids test the most competitive spirits. They put in near the C & O Canal right across from Old Angler's Inn, a tavern and restaurant since 1860. It's a pricey spot to take a break, but you may need the energy for the hill leading to the entrance to Great

Falls Park. It's a long climb, so gear down and pedal easy to enjoy the smoothly-paved road through deep woods.

Stay left at the top and zoom down the other side of the same hill to arrive at the Great Falls Tavern Visitor Center. Be sure to stop at the guard house—there's an entrance fee of $2 for cyclists and $4 for cars. The tavern was built in 1890 to serve workers on the C & O Canal. Today it is a museum. Just across the canal, footpaths and platforms present views of this ferocious section of river, where in 0.25 mile rapids drop 76 feet through a gorge. Ask a local to point out the bald-eagle nest on a river island.

Decision time: Either climb the steep hill back out of the park to double back to D.C. on the MacArthur Boulevard trail, or return on the C & O Canal towpath, described in ride 13.

Note: In January 1996 a major flood breached the canal and ravaged its towpath. As this edition goes to press, sections of the canal have been closed by the National Park Service and will not be accessible for several months. Call the Great Falls Tavern Visitor's Center at (301) 299-3613 for up-to-date information.

Upper Reaches of Rock Creek Park

Distance:	7.8-mile loop
Approximate pedaling time:	1 hour
Terrain:	Very hilly
Surface:	Two-lane roads and off-road trails
Things to see:	Natural areas of Rock Creek Park
Option:	Connection to Maryland bike path

Washington cyclists can take a midweek break in the country without leaving the city limits. This can be accomplished by touring the looping road system of northern Rock Creek Park.

This is Rock Creek's more rustic side. The park's 1,800 acres are 85 percent wooded and contain fifteen wildflower meadows comprising 400 plant species, including goldenrod, purpletop grass, thistle, and aster. A British ambassador once asked rhetorically, "What city in the world is there where a man can, within a quarter of an hour and on his own feet, get in a beautiful rocky glen such as you would find in the woods of Maine or Scotland?" Here Theodore Roosevelt would go off on rugged jaunts, and John Quincy Adams described visiting "this romantic glen, listening to the singing of a thousand birds."

Among the glades and dells of Rock Creek are great stands of tulip trees, oak, and dogwood, with an understory of alder bush, azalea, and witch hazel. The park roads have been designed to follow the undulations of these hills. Dramatic, sweeping curves provide excellent views of the gorge. Bridle paths cross the road beds at many intervals. Traffic is light except on Beach Drive, a busy commuter road on weekdays that is closed to motor traffic on weekends and holidays (see Ride 4). An off-road trail runs parallel to the portion of Beach Drive included in this ride.

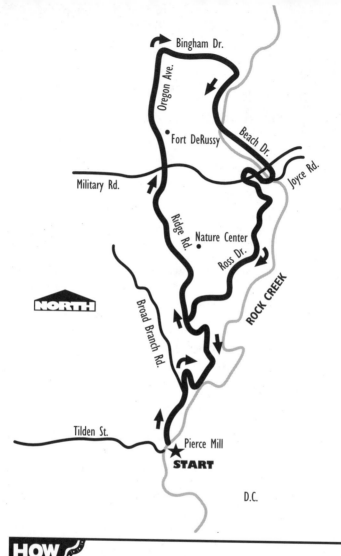

Bingham Dr.

Oregon Ave.

Fort DeRussy

Beach Dr.

Joyce Rd.

Military Rd.

Ridge Rd.

Nature Center

Ross Dr.

ROCK CREEK

NORTH

Broad Branch Rd.

Tilden St.

Pierce Mill
START

D.C.

HOW to get there Heading south on Connecticut Avenue, turn left on Tilden Street to Pierce Mill. From Virginia, take Rock Creek Parkway south to Pierce Mill. Heading north on Connecticut Avenue, turn right on Tilden Street to Pierce Mill.

DIRECTIONS for the ride

- Head north from Pierce Mill parking area.
- In 0.25 mile, left on Broad Branch Road and immediate right onto Ridge Road.
- Bear left at sign for Nature Center as Ross Road turns right.
- At Military Road traffic light, go straight. Ridge Road becomes Oregon Avenue.
- Right on Bingham Drive.
- Right on off-road trail parallel to Beach Drive.
- At four-way stop, right on Joyce Road.
- First left on Ross Drive.
- Ross Drive ends at Ridge Road near Nature Center. Turn left.
- Left at bottom of long hill.
- Right into Pierce Mill parking area.

Start next to the rumbling falls at historic Pierce Mill. Proceed north through the parking area with Rock Creek on your right. In 0.25 mile, turn left onto two-lane Broad Branch Road and take an immediate right on Ridge Road. Climb a steep hill for 0.5 mile. Note the rustic stone wall on the S-curve. Pass a rambling meadow retained by a split-log fence.

Bear left at a sign for the Nature Center to traverse a broad meadow with playing fields and picnic tables. Come to an intersection with a traffic light. Cross four-lane Military Road (an important Civil War supply line) to reach Oregon Avenue. (Or take the marked, off-road path that runs parallel.) This two-lane road divides a residential neighborhood from the dense woods of Rock Creek Park's western border. The rambling houses on the left are among the city's most exclusive, combining bucolic pleasures with a short commute to downtown D.C. On the right are the ruins of Fort DeRussy at the park's highest point. A hike into the woods will reveal the remains of earthworks, moats, and trenches from this Civil War site.

At Bingham Drive turn right and hang on for a steep descent down to the Rock Creek basin. You can choose between the road bed

(smooth surface, no shoulders, moderate traffic) or the path at left (separate from traffic, fair surface). At Beach Drive, to avoid heavy traffic, turn right onto a much smoother off-road trail. Continue along the valley floor for about 1 mile to Joyce Road, a four-way stop. Turn right and immediately left on Ross Drive. Prepare for several steep climbs and descents through wooded highlands. Near the Nature Center, Ross Drive melts into Ridge Road. Like all good rides, this one ends with a sharp descent. Slow down for the S-curve around a picnic meadow, and return to Pierce Mill.

Option: To connect to Rock Creek Regional Park in Maryland, keep straight on Oregon rather than turning right on Bingham Drive. Follow Oregon until it ends at Western Avenue, and turn left. Shortly thereafter turn right on Greenvale Street. In a few blocks, turn left on Beach Drive. Cross the bridge at Candy Cane City, a playground next to the Meadowbrook Riding Stables, to reach the Maryland bikeway through Rock Creek Regional Park, described in ride 4. It runs about 13 miles to Lake Needwood.

Sligo–Rock Creek Weekend Loop

Distance:	11-mile loop
Approximate pedaling time:	90 minutes
Terrain:	Hilly
Things to see:	Rock Creek Park, Walter Reed Annex, historic Forest Glen, Sligo Creek Park, Takoma Park

Think quick escape. If you live in D.C., Bethesda, Silver Spring, or Takoma Park, you can do this ride without loading the roof rack or jumping on the subway. This is my after-gardening-but-before-dinner ride. Combining aspects of Rides 11 and 14, it melds routes through two stream-valley parks with looks at two historic areas not covered elsewhere here. It's a weekend-only ride because it includes sections of Beach Drive that are closed to cars Saturday and Sunday but packed with commuters on weekdays.

Start at the intersection of Beach and Sherrill drives in the D.C. portion of Rock Creek Park, about 2 miles north of the National Zoo. Head north past picnic areas, rock outcroppings, and stands of mountain laurel (the white blooms come out in late May). Horse trails parallel this route, along with hiking trails maintained by the Potomac Appalachian Trail Club. Lock up your bike sometime and try one— it's easy to lose the city within the park's 1,800 acres.

Most but not all of Beach Drive is closed on weekends, but a few sections remain open so groups can reach picnic areas by car; beware of the occasional auto. After leaving the city through a bikes-only gate, look for a playground called Candy Cane City. A marked sign on the right leads off Beach Drive and over a small bridge. Turn left

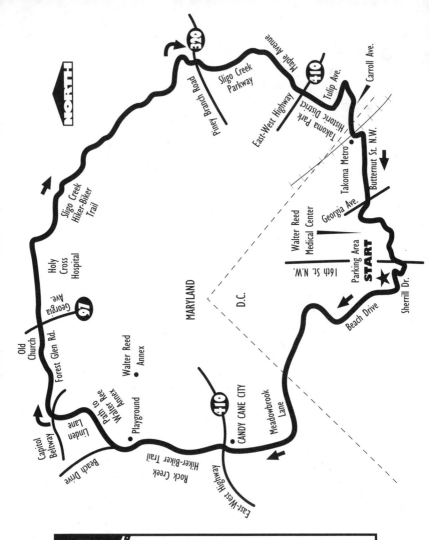

HOW to get there From the south, head north on Rock Creek Parkway and follow signs for Beach Drive/National Zoo. Stay on Beach Drive and park in picnic areas just before or after Sherrill Drive on the right. Coming crosstown, take Military Road to the Beach Drive/Ross Drive exit.

- From Sherrill Drive, right on Beach Drive to head north.
- From Beach Drive, turn right to enter Candy Cane City playground. Bear left and follow bike route signs out of parking lot.
- Left at T onto Meadowbrook Lane.

- Cross East-West Highway (Route 410) to pick up Rock Creek bike path north.
- Turn right past small playground to take path to Walter Reed Annex.
- Left on Linden Lane.
- Follow bike route signs across Beltway and railroad tracks.
- At top of hill, where sign reads BIKE ROUTE ENDS (ignore it), go straight to pick up Forest Glen Road through historic Forest Glen.
- Cross Georgia Avenue at signal to stay on Forest Glen Road for another six blocks.
- After passing Holy Cross Hospital on right, turn right onto Sligo Creek Hiker-Biker Trail.
- Ride 3.5 miles to end of trail at Piney Branch Road.
- After crossing Piney Branch at signal, go straight onto Sligo Creek Parkway (caution—narrow road with traffic).
- At T, right on Maple Avenue.
- At 4-way stop, left on Tulip Avenue.
- In 3 blocks at T, right on Carroll Avenue.
- At Takoma clock tower, turn right to stay on Carroll Avenue. Stay on Carroll through underpass beneath Metrorail tracks.
- Left onto Fourth Street N.W. at signal immediately after underpass.
- In one block, right onto Butternut Street N.W.
- At Georgia Avenue, cross at signal to enter gates of Walter Reed Medical Center.
- Exit Walter Reed at Alaska Avenue gate.
- Left on Alaska Avenue N.W.
- Left on Sixteenth Street (traffic).
- First right on Sherrill Drive. Return to start.

into a parking lot and pass the playground and ball fields until you reach a T next to a horse pasture; this is the Meadowbrook Stable. Turn left on Meadowbrook Lane until you come to East-West Highway, a major arterial. Cross at the signal to pick up a bike path that heads north past playing fields and wetlands. Proceed to the Walter Reed Annex as described in Ride 4 (Rock Creek Park: D.C. to Maryland and Back). This time you'll pass through the architectural theme park. At the top of the bike path, turn left onto Linden Lane and bear right at the next fork (signed bike route).

Coast down a hill (past Ye Forest Inne, a failed resort in the 1890s and now part of Walter Reed Annex) to cross the Beltway on an overpass and cruise through the historic community of Forest Glen. Founded by the notable Carroll family in the 1700s among a 4,200-acre tract of wilderness, Forest Glen retains a country feel, with winding roads and old frame houses with broad porches. On the left St. John's Cemetery doubles as a village green. The road is tight, but the drivers courteous. At the top of the hill are railroad tracks and the former B & O railroad station.

After passing the new Forest Glen Metrorail station, cross busy Georgia Avenue at the signal and descend past Holy Cross Hospital on the right. Bear right at the bottom of the hill to pick up the Sligo Creek Hiker-Biker trail.

Environmentally speaking, Sligo Creek has long been a poor sister to the wider, better preserved Rock Creek valley, but that may be changing. (It's hard to believe that the sometimes foul-smelling Sligo supplied water mains until 1930.) The local sewer commission plans to remove leaky pipes (think the worst) from the creek bed to a new right-of-way above the banks. Many new trees, including lovely paperbark birches, have been planted in the park, and wildflower meadows have supplanted boring expanses of lawn. Parts of the creek banks are being restored with native vegetation, and the number of fish species living in Sligo Creek is expected to jump from one to a dozen or so. Best yet, there are plans to extend the hiker-biker trail 3.3 miles east, where it will meet the trailhead of Northwest Branch (see Ride 21).

Roll through this part of the trail until it ends at Piney Branch

Road. But more good news here. À la Beach Drive, the Piney Branch–Maple Avenue stretch of Sligo Creek Parkway is now closed to cars most Sundays. Ride on the parkway until Maple Avenue, then turn right to pass by Takoma Park's high-rise apartment district. This section ends at the Sam Abbott Municipal Center, named for the late rabble-rousing mayor, a socialist who fought proposed highways that would have destroyed Takoma Park. He once said, "It doesn't bother me at all that I don't have suburban decorum." Next door is a friendly city library—the only one in Maryland outside of Baltimore.

Go straight to enter the Takoma Park Historic District. Founded in 1976 in the wake of highway and other development battles, the historic district embraces parts of D.C. and two Maryland counties. The city was carved out of farms and wilderness in 1883 by developer Benjamin Franklin Gilbert; in 1904 it took off in a spurt when the Seventh-Day Adventist church moved from Battle Creek, Michigan, to make Takoma its headquarters. (SDA has moved to sober corporate headquarters in Silver Spring, leaving in its righteous wake an almost publess, dry Takoma.)

A ride up Maple Avenue reveals large, four-square homes mixed in with gingerbread Victorians dating back to the 1890s. Many have been restored. An original city boundary marker (c. 1791) sits behind an iron fence near Maple and Carroll avenues. Turn left down Tulip Avenue to the main drag, Carroll Avenue. Here is the heart of Washington's "folk ghetto," the House of Musical Traditions, where you can buy a hammered dulcimer or take lessons in African drumming, along with other craft shops, book stores, and restaurants. A Sunday farmers' market (in season) makes a cycling destination—bring panniers.

Follow Carroll Avenue (Route 195) as it turns right toward the Takoma Metro station. Take Butternut Street N.W. in D.C. At Georgia Avenue go straight through the gates for a tour of the Walter Reed Army Medical Center, founded in 1898. This formal campus mixes Georgian architecture with modern and features one major public attraction: the National Museum of Health and Medicine, repository of the bullet that killed Lincoln, along with other medical curios and scientific exhibits. Until the late sixties this was one of the most popular museums on the Mall; to make room for the Hirshhorn Museum, the red brick building was razed and the collection exiled to Walter Reed.

After winding through the Reed complex, take Sixteenth Street south to Sherrill Drive. Head downhill to return to the ride's starting point.

National Arboretum Loop-de-Loop

Distance:	9-mile loop
Approximate pedaling time:	1 hour
Terrain:	Very hilly
Surface:	Smooth roads
Things to see:	Bonsai collection, azalea garden, U.S. Capitol columns, Anacostia River, ponds and streams

Washington has long been known as the "City of Trees." Most neighborhoods are lined by oaks, sycamores, or even ginkgo trees, and the April blooming of the Japanese cherry trees draws millions of tourists. But the most impressive year-round display can be found at the 444-acre National Arboretum in the midst of gritty Northeast Washington. Here the prevailing mood falls between virgin forest and formal garden. Many of the trees, shrubs, and herbs are so rare they attract visitors from throughout the world.

Founded in 1927 under the auspices of the U.S. Department of Agriculture, the arboretum blooms from March through October. In winter the colors become considerably more muted, but the collection of dwarf conifers, the frozen ponds, and the tall wheat-colored grasses make off-season visits worthwhile. Summer visitors are rewarded by the sight of vast lily pads with their pink and white blooms. Ostensibly a research facility for botanists, the arboretum is one of the more graceful and serene parks in Washington.

This suggested tour loops around the grounds three times to cover most of its 9 miles of lightly traveled roads. Many are unmarked, so you may find it difficult to follow this route exactly. All the roads are bikeable, though. If you miss a turn, just follow the signs back to the gift shop.

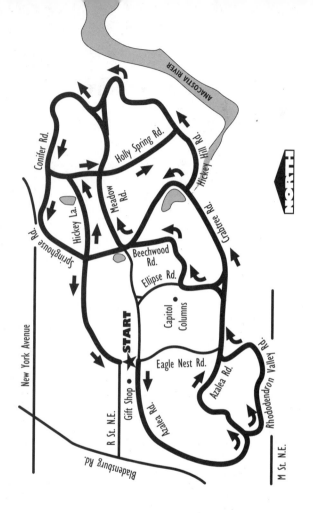

NORTH

ANACOSTIA RIVER

Conifer Rd.
Holly Spring Rd.
Hickey Hill Rd.
Meadow Rd.
Crabtree Rd.
Hickey La.
Springhouse Rd.
Beechwood Rd.
Ellipse Rd.
Capitol Columns
START
New York Avenue
Gift Shop
Eagle Nest Rd.
Azalea Rd.
Azalea Rd.
Rhododendron Valley Rd.
R St. N.E.
Bladensburg Rd.
M St. N.E.

HOW to get there From Capitol Hill, take Maryland Avenue to M Street entrance. From downtown, take New York Avenue to service road on right after Bladensburg Road. From Maryland, take Route 50 West to New York Avenue and follow signs to service road. Park at information center and gift shop.

DIREC-TIONS for the ride

- By bike, head west on Azalea Road past gift shop.
- At Rhododendron Valley Road, bear left to stay on Azalea Road.
- Azalea Road becomes Crabtree Road.
- At pond, bear right on Hickey Hill Road.
- At Y intersection, bear right on Conifer Road.
- At Y intersection, bear left and then right on Hickey Lane. Return to start.
- Head west on Azalea Road.
- At pond, bear left on Valley Road.
- Right on Meadow Road.
- Bear left at Y intersection.
- Left on Conifer Road and return to start.
- West on Azalea Road.
- Left on Ellipse Road to see U.S. Capitol columns.
- Right on Beechwood Road.
- Right on Meadow Road.
- Left on Holly Spring Road.
- Left on Conifer Road and return to start.

The ride starts near the National Bonsai Collection. Housed in a Japanese-style pavilion, the bonsai trees are up to 350 years old but only a few feet high. Their disposition results from generations of careful "training" by Japanese horticulturists, who donated their life's work in honor of our bicentennial. These tiny ginkgoes, maples, spruces, and crab apples form an alluring landscape in miniature.

Starting just past the gift shop at the entrance, the ride begins with a steep climb up to a precipice with a view of the mausoleums of a historic cemetery across Bladensburg Road. In spring the 65,000 azaleas on this hillock burst out in pink, purple, orange, and scarlet blooms. There's also a stand of a type of dawn redwood that exists nowhere else outside of China. Cruising downhill at high speed, pass flowering crab apples and a bird garden. The road continues to de-

scend into a dark valley of ferns. Cross a stream bed and bear right at a pond (often full of geese) to climb again for a view of the Anacostia River. This slow-moving tidal branch of the Potomac is here seen at its bucolic best.

Heading north, the cyclist encounters Japanese, Korean, and Chinese gardens complemented by pagodas, bridges, and other structures of the East. A cruise past neat rows of Japanese maples completes the first leg. Starting again from the parking area, repeat the first section of the ride until reaching Beech Spring Pond, where you turn left instead of bearing right. Near a second pond, by a fragrant area of lilacs and hibiscus, turn right to cross a broad meadow. Take the next two left turns to traverse what looks like pristine farmland on the way back to the start.

The final leg affords a look at a hillside planted with 1,500 dwarf conifers such as yew, cedar, and pine. Like the bonsai, the dwarf conifers have been sculpted into shapely miniatures. Unlike the potted Japanese trees, they are planted in the ground, giving the impression of a troll forest. Another quirky feature on the grounds is the collection of the original Corinthian columns from the east portico of the U.S. Capitol. The columns were dismantled in the 1950s when the east front was remodeled. They were only recently re-erected in their original configuration—freestanding columns eerily girding nothing. The latest addition to the arboretum is a collection of bonsai trained in North America. Two projects are on the boards: a National Bird Garden and a National Grove of State Trees.

Except in spring, when the azaleas burst, the arboretum is never as crowded as other Washington attractions. The roads all run one-way. Since most people walk the grounds, you won't encounter many automobiles. The only drawback is that the arboretum is not easily reached by bike paths, on-road routes, or Metrorail.

C & O Canal
Georgetown to Great Falls

Distance:	15 miles, one-way
Approximate pedaling time:	2 hours
Terrain:	Flat
Surface:	Packed dirt with some rocks
Things to see:	Working locks of nineteenth-century canal, rapids and dams of Potomac River, lockkeepers' houses and other historic structures
Facilities:	Rest room, snacks, bike and canoe rentals, fishing gear at Fletcher's Boat House and Swain's Lock; snacks and boat rides at Great Falls
Option:	Extend ride to Seneca, Maryland; return via MacArthur Boulevard; join ride 26; join ride 25

The Chesapeake & Ohio Canal was destined to be a financial flop even before the first spadeful of earth was turned in 1828. The reason: the rise of railroads. By 1850, when canal construction stretched 184 miles from Georgetown in Washington to Cumberland, Maryland, in the Appalachian Mountains, freight trains had siphoned away much of the canal's business.

In 1924 the obsolete canal closed for good. In the 1950s even the *Washington Post* advocated filling in the remains to create a new commuter road. In stepped U.S. Supreme Court Justice William O. Douglas, an avid birder and hiker who led a cavalcade of decision-makers on a nature walk that changed many minds. In 1977 President Jimmy

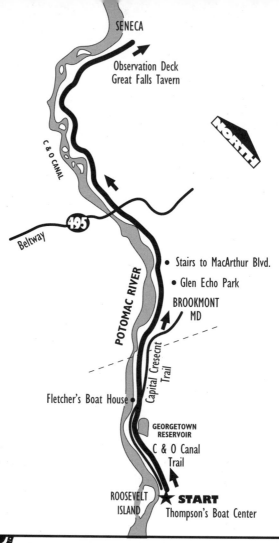

SENECA

Observation Deck
Great Falls Tavern

NORTH

C & O CANAL

495

Beltway

• Stairs to MacArthur Blvd.
• Glen Echo Park

BROOKMONT
MD

POTOMAC RIVER

Capital Crescent Trail

Fletcher's Boat House •

GEORGETOWN
RESERVOIR

C & O Canal
Trail

ROOSEVELT
ISLAND

★ START
Thompson's Boat Center

HOW
to get
there
From north, Rock Creek Parkway to Thompson's parking lot;
turn right. From the Mall, Virginia Avenue west across Rock
Creek Parkway to Thompson's parking lot. From Virginia,
Theodore Roosevelt or Memorial Bridge to Rock Creek Parkway to
Thompson's parking lot. By Metro, Blue or Orange Line to Foggy
Bottom/GWU, about 1-mile walk via New Hampshire and Virginia
avenues.

DIREC-TIONS for the ride

- Exit Thompson's Boat Center toward Rock Creek Parkway.
- Turn left immediately on Rock Creek bike path.
- After crossing concrete bridge, turn left on brick trail. This is trailhead for towpath of C & O Canal.
- After crossing Twenty-eighth and Twenty-ninth streets in George-town, trail becomes packed dirt.
- At Thirty-fourth Street, cross footbridge to other side of canal. Trail continues on Potomac River side.
- Follow milestones to Great Falls. Note: Cyclists must dismount and walk near Great Falls for about a quarter mile.

Options: You may return via the route described in ride 10 by taking the park road up the hill out of Great Falls. At top of hill, turn right onto MacArthur Boulevard.

You may join ride 26 by continuing on the towpath to White's Ferry, Maryland.

You may join ride 25 by continuing past Great Falls to Pennyfield Lock Road. Turn right on Pennyfield, climb a hill, and turn left on River Road.

Carter dedicated the C & O Canal National Historical Park in honor of Douglas.

The route follows the unpaved towpath, designed for mules to pull oblong barges carrying coal down the canal. Though bumpy in places (skinny tires, beware), the path offers many rewards for cyclists, joggers, and birders. Today mules still pull replicas of the old canal barges for pleasure rides down the canal. Injecting a linear slice of nature right into the city, the canal is lined by a canopy of sycamore, red maple, sassafras, and willow trees, along with wild-flowers such as blue phlox, Queen Anne's lace, and may-apples, mushrooms, and wild raspberry. The bird density is three times that of the regional average. While pedaling my mountain bike at 15 miles per hour, I've spotted barred owls, pileated woodpeckers, red-tailed hawks, and bluebirds. Spouts that bypass the locks create little falls rumbling over boulders. Turnarounds for barges have degraded into freshwater swamps full of cattails and hawk roosts. The still, opaque waters of the canal itself are alive with carp and turtles.

Canal cruisers will begin their rides at the Harry T. Thompson Boat Center, the starting point for many rides described in this book. Turn left out of the parking lot and left again onto a brick path marked as the beginning of the C & O park. Passing through Georgetown, you'll encounter the first canal lock. This begins a ride to Great Falls headed ever-so-slightly uphill—a total of 190 feet in 15 miles. The entire route is restored with working locks and charming field-stone lockkeepers' houses. Brown mile-markers along the way make it easy to find canal highlights and ruins.

For example:

• Mile 0: The towpath passes under the grand arches of Key Bridge. Francis Scott Key actually lived near here in a mansion dismantled in the 1940s. A footpath leads up to M Street and the many shops and historic houses of the old port of Georgetown.

• Mile 0.1: Next to a vast green boathouse in Georgetown, find the remains of the Old Alexandria Aqueduct, which spanned the Potomac. This is also the starting point for the new Capital Crescent Trail, which follows an old railroad right-of-way to downtown Bethesda. See Ride 5 for a complete loop incorporating this rail-to-trail stretch.

• Mile 1.8: Look across the Potomac for a view of a wet-weather waterfall on the Virginia side.

• Mile 2.4: Another boathouse with a country flavor, Fletcher's, rents mountain bikes, boats, and fishing gear.

• Mile 2.7: Pass under the old B & O railroad bridge, which now carries the Capital Crescent Trail away from the river, across the canal.

• Mile 4.7: The "feeder" draws water from the river to discharge into the canal at lock 5. Look closely at the curved red sandstone of the locks to find initials and symbols carved in by the stone cutters.

• Mile 6.6: A 0.5-mile walking path connects the towpath to Glen Echo Park, described in Ride 10.

• Mile 7.3: Pass under the 220-foot-long arch of the Cabin John Bridge, an engineering marvel of the 1850s.

• Mile 12.6: Enter Widewater, a broad section of the canal that looks like a mountain lake. The going gets a bit rough for a quarter mile where you may have to walk your bike over rocks and boulders.

• Mile 15: Arrive at Great Falls Tavern, a hostelry built in 1831 and restored in 1942. Today the whitewashed structure houses a museum. Be sure to view the spectacular falls from the platform. From this location, looking 20 degrees to the right, you can spot an active bald-eagle nest spreading out among the high branches of a sycamore. It's on the banks of a river island.

Option: The length of this ride will satisfy most cyclists, but if you want to explore the canal further, you can ride another 7 miles to Seneca Creek. The creek is close to several old quarries from which the stone for the Smithsonian castle was pulled. Points of interest en route include Swain's Lock, the site of an old lockkeeper's house now used to rent canoes and bikes and sell snacks. After Pennyfield lock, site of the ruins of historic Tobytown, the river grows quite wide. Just up to the left, a bottomland marsh has been designated a waterfowl sanctuary. It's full of wildflowers, fish, and herons as well as ducks and geese.

The quality of the towpath surface degenerates after Seneca Creek. Although riding the entire 184-mile route (with detours and overnight stops) is a popular "once-in-a-lifetime" experience, the Georgetown-Seneca route offers years' worth of exploration. I've yet to exhaust my interest.

Note: In January 1996 a major flood breached the canal and ravaged its towpath. As this edition goes to press, sections of the canal have been closed by the National Park Service and will not be accessible for several months. Call the Great Falls Tavern Visitor's Center at (301) 299-3613 for up-to-date information.

Tour of South Arlington

Distance:	17-mile loop
Approximate pedaling time:	2 hours
Terrain:	Rolling
Surface:	Excellent off-road trail with center stripe, boardwalk, ramps, and bridges
Things to see:	"Contemporary urban development," wildflower meadow, bird sanctuary, pretty neighborhoods, creek, and Potomac shores
Facilities:	Rest rooms, parks, and water fountains en route

At 25.7 square miles, Arlington is the smallest county in the United States, but it has resolved to become one of the best municipalities for cycling, with more than 75 miles of trails and on-street routes. Arlington's reputation as a cycling mecca was solidified in 1989 with the Virginia debut of the Tour duPont, America's biggest pro cycling race. Former Tour de France winner Greg Lemond and other world-class riders contested a stage of this two-week race along the George Washington Parkway.

Though the area that is now Arlington was discovered by Captain John Smith in 1607 and first mapped out as part of the District of Columbia in 1791, it remained unsettled for much longer. Small farms arrived only around 1850, and government workers in search of suburbs to settle came around 1910. Farms and log cabins could be found within its boundaries into this century. Well before all that, the original inhabitants were probably the Doegs and Necostins of the Algonquin tribes. Today's Arlington is a rapidly developing area with

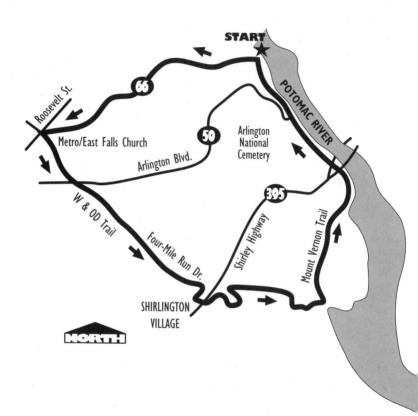

START

POTOMAC RIVER

66

Roosevelt St.

Metro/East Falls Church

50

Arlington Blvd.

Arlington National Cemetery

395

W & OD Trail

Four-Mile Run Dr.

Shirley Highway

Mount Vernon Trail

SHIRLINGTON VILLAGE

NORTH

HOW to get there From Georgetown, cross Key Bridge to the intersection of Lee Highway and Fort Myer Drive. Turn right on Lee Highway and follow signs to Interstate 66. From Alexandria, take Mount Vernon path north to National Airport and begin loop there. By Metro, take Blue or Orange Line to Rosslyn; then take Wilson Boulevard east to Lee Highway and Fort Myer Drive.

DIREC-TIONS for the ride

- From intersection of Fort Myer Drive and Lee Highway, pick up Interstate-66 trail by riding on sidewalk next to Lee Highway until you reach brick Air Force Association building. Trail begins here, behind a concrete sound barrier.
- West for 5 miles on trail.
- Trail ends at North Kennebec Street. Left onto Four-Mile Run trail. (To head to East Falls Church Metrorail station, turn right on Four-Mile Run trail and head 1 mile to East Falls Church Park, then right on North Roosevelt.)
- On Four-Mile Run path, head northeast under Arlington and Wilson boulevards and Walter Reed Drive.
- Near Interstate 395, right on South Randolph Street and left on South Twenty-eighth Street.
- Pedestrian overpass across Interstate 395 (Shirley Highway).
- Left on Custis Road.
- Left on West Glebe Road. Use sidewalk to reach South Glebe Road, which leads to Wayne F. Anderson Bikeway (poorly marked).
- Follow sidewalk over Route 1 to passage under railroad tracks leading to Mount Vernon Trail.
- Left on Mount Vernon trail. Follow signs to Rosslyn and take path under Memorial Bridge (rather than bearing left, which will divert you across the George Washington Parkway toward Arlington Cemetery—see Ride 1).

about 140,000 residents. Charming and historic bungalow neighborhoods stand cheek-by-jowl with new high rises and highways.

An off-road tour of Arlington begins in Rosslyn, the high-rise district (and home of *USA Today*) just across the river from historic Georgetown. A trip down the interstate will take you into the heart of the county.

Along with parts of Route 70 in Colorado, the new section of Interstate 66 through Arlington is one of the few interstate highways in the United States that not only allows but encourages cycling. Like its Rocky Mountain counterpart, Interstate 66 features a well-thought-out multi-use trail made possible by spectacular engineering. The path soars well above the road bed on buff-colored concrete barriers that also muffle road noise from the adjoining neighborhoods and crisscrosses the four-lane road on high ramps and bridges. The grades are surprisingly steep and frequent. It's a trip through a manufactured mountain range that I call the Concrete Cotswolds.

That said, the route (also known officially as the Custis Memorial Trail) is darned handy. Its many direct connections include Key Bridge into Georgetown, the new Theodore Roosevelt Island Pedestrian/Bicycle Bridge leading to the Mount Vernon trail, the W & OD trail, and the Four-Mile Run trail. It's also the middle link for an uninterrupted 64-mile off-road ride through northern Virginia (which can be extended by crossing into Washington or Maryland).

Moreover, the Interstate-66 trail is practical. Connections to at least a dozen neighborhoods and commercial areas allow residents to commute or shop without a car. The signs on the trail point you exactly where you're going; for a change, they're at least as good as the road signs.

All this came about as a result of a twenty-five-year battle to build Interstate 66, originally conceived as an eight-lane superhighway. Neighborhood groups sued to save their homes and trees, while the highway engineers compromised by cutting back on auto lanes, adding a median for Metrorail, planning parks and sound barriers, and designing this impressive bike byway. Opposition never dissolved entirely, but the road did get built.

About the only thing lacking along Interstate 66 is scenery. Mostly you see banal high-rises, zooming autos, and plastic-looking plantings. It does, however, get you to where you're going, the much more bucolic Four-Mile Run trail, which meets at a wildflower meadow at Interstate 66 near the Beltway and the East Falls Church Metrorail station.

Four-Mile Run forms the second side of a triangular route around Arlington. The creek serves as the natural border between Arlington County and Alexandria City. Close by its southern section you can find an original D.C. boundary marker, an old quarry, a meadow preserve, and the remains of an old bungalow-and-cottage neighborhood that was divided by highway construction. The path is broad and smooth and is bisected by a dotted yellow line, which should be standard equipment on all trails. Head along the creek's south bank into Bon Air Park, where there is a rose garden well worth seeing in season.

Continue through a valley into Glen Carlyn Park, which blooms with mountain laurel, dogwood, and azalea in spring. A waterfall marks the location of an old mill. Excursion steam trains once stopped here to pick up water for their locomotives. This is Arlington's own fall line, signifying the end of the coastal plain and the commencement of the Piedmont Plateau. George Washington once surveyed the site. Look for a historical marker. More history: Near South Fourth Street, just off the trail, is the 1742 Ball-Sellers House, once owned by George Washington's tailor.

After crossing under Arlington Boulevard, the route bifurcates into low and high roads. The high road offers vistas, but the low road (actually part of the W & OD trail) is much safer. After passing through a broad forest, you exit not into a meadow but into a very urban area, replete with a fording of Interstate 395.

On the other side of 395 is Shirlington Village, a former strip shopping mall that has been reconstituted as a "neotraditional" development that's supposed to recall an old-fashioned brick-lined Main Street. It's a place to stroll or have an ice-cream cone, and there's a bike shop on the main drag. Pick up the trail again until Four-Mile Run drains into the Potomac, near a rail yard and National Airport. At this transportation nexus, turn left onto the Mount Vernon Trail, which takes you safely back to Rosslyn by way of Arlington Cemetery and Roosevelt Island.

Tour of North Arlington

Distance:	10 miles
Approximate pedaling time:	1 hour
Terrain:	Rolling
Surface:	Well-maintained suburban roads and off-road bike paths
Things to see:	Gulf Branch Nature Center and Potomac Overlook Regional Park
Facilities:	Rest rooms at Potomac Overlook Regional Park
Option:	Connection to C & O Canal towpath (Ride 14) and Capital Crescent Loop (Ride 5) via Chain Bridge

You live in North Arlington and are looking for a short, fun ride you can fit into a busy schedule. Or you'd like to know an easy way across Chain Bridge so you can follow the C & O towpath into Georgetown for brunch, out to Great Falls for a picnic, or even to Bethesda via the new Capital Crescent Trail. Or maybe you live on the Maryland side of the Potomac and would like to explore a little bit of Arlington.

Here's a convenient ride that loops around Arlington's suburban highlands, perched high above the Potomac River in the county's northern corner. It connects a few very rideable artery roads with a stream-side bike path to form a simple 10-mile loop.

Start at Potomac Overlook Regional Park, which features tennis courts, playing fields, and a picnic area.

Exit the park via Marcy Road and turn right onto Military Road. At the bottom of the hill, where the road narrows to two lanes, turn left to cross Military Road (carefully!) and follow the bike path that

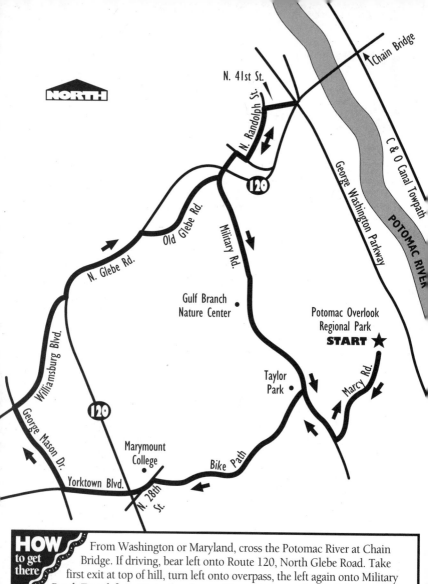

NORTH

N. 41st St.

Chain Bridge

N. Randolph St.

120

C & O Canal Towpath

POTOMAC RIVER

George Washington Parkway

Old Glebe Rd.

N. Glebe Rd.

Military Rd.

Gulf Branch
Nature Center

Potomac Overlook
Regional Park
START ★

Williamsburg Blvd.

120

Taylor
Park

Marcy Rd.

George Mason Dr.

Marymount
College

Bike Path

Yorktown Blvd.

N. 28th St.

HOW to get there From Washington or Maryland, cross the Potomac River at Chain Bridge. If driving, bear left onto Route 120, North Glebe Road. Take first exit at top of hill, turn left onto overpass, the left again onto Military Road. Turn left on Marcy Road to parking at Potomac Overlook Regional Park. If bicycling from Chain Bridge, ride uphill on Forty-first Street immediately after crossing river. Continue at dead-end onto steep bike path, then turn left on North Randolph Street to access Route 120 overpass and Military Road.

DIREC-TIONS for the ride

- Exit Potomac Overlook Regional Park on Marcy Road.
- Right onto Military Road.
- At bottom of long hill, where Military narrows to two lanes, dismount and walk your bike across Military. Here, at Taylor Park, follow a narrow bike path into the woods.
- Continue on bike path as it crosses North Vernon Street.
- Left onto North 28th Street, directly across from Marymount College, at the bike path's end.
- Immediate right onto Yorktown Boulevard, which passes beneath North Glebe Road.
- Right on George Mason Drive. At dead end, continue straight onto short bike path leading to separate section of George Mason.
- Right on Williamsburg Boulevard.
- Left on North Glebe Road (Route 120) at traffic light.
- Right on Old Glebe Road at white church.
- Right on Military Road. (Or, to access Chain Bridge, continue straight onto the overpass and follow the directions under "Option" below.)
- Left on Marcy Road to start/finish at Potomac Overlook Regional Park.

Option: To connect this ride with the C & O Canal towpath via Chain Bridge, follow Old Glebe Road straight onto the overpass over North Glebe instead of turning right on Military Road. Bear right on the other side, then turn left onto North Randolph Street. Look for a bike path entrance on the right—it's next to a log-cabin-style house—and follow it down a steep stretch to North 41st Street and a small parking area. Follow the marked bike lane through a busy intersection and directly onto the protected sidewalk across the bridge. On the Maryland side of the bridge, there's a hiker–biker ramp providing direct access to the canal towpath. Turn left to head in the direction of Great Falls, or right to reach Georgetown or the Capital Crescent Trail.

leads off into the woods. The path alternates between hard-packed dirt and pavement as it winds its way up this narrow, wooded watershed.

Emerge from the trees, and return to regular roads, across from Marymount College. Turn left onto North 28th Street, and then immediately right onto Yorktown Boulevard. Following a few up-and-down blocks through this well-kept neighborhood, turn right onto George Mason Drive. Cars would face a dead end here, but you can continue straight onto the short section of bike path that crosses a stream and connects to another stretch of George Mason Drive. Ride on for a few more blocks, then turn right onto Williamsburg Boulevard.

Williamsburg, following a short steep hill, ends at a stop light. Turn left here onto North Glebe Road, Route 120, which leads to Chain Bridge. Rather than follow this road all the way to the river, turn right onto Old Glebe Road at the big white church. This original route to the river passes by some nice, older cottages before connecting with Military Road.

Turn right onto Military to return to Marcy Road. On the way, stop and explore Gulf Branch Nature Center. You can park your bikes here and follow a narrow ravine trail down to the shore of the Potomac. This is a favorite spot for fishing or for just viewing the river up close.

For views from a higher vantage point, explore Potomac Overlook Park's network of short trails. But not by bike—Arlington is cyclist-friendly, as this ride will have shown, but these trails are for hikers only.

17 Neighborhoods of Northwest D.C.

Distance:	13-mile loop
Approximate pedaling time:	2 hours
Terrain:	Hilly
Surface:	City roads, potholes and all
Things to see:	Historic Logan Circle, row-house neighborhoods, Fort Stevens, Takoma Park, Gold Coast, lower Rock Creek Park, Dupont Circle
Option:	Trip to downtown Takoma Park farmer's market

Here's a ride that takes you through a part of Washington that tourists never see—the places beyond the monuments where people actually live. The route meanders through row-house neighborhoods both historic and of more recent vintage. Catch a bit of Takoma Park's New Age funk before visiting the site where the South almost won the Civil War, then see one of the capital's premier upper-middle-class neighborhoods before swinging through Rock Creek Park to urbane Dupont Circle.

Let me add a caveat: This route is for a special breed of rider—the city biker. These intrepid pedalers don't mind dressing from head to toe in canary yellow, painting their helmets blaze orange, installing expensive puncture-proof tubes, or occasionally sharing an eight-foot-wide street with an eight-foot-wide bus. They seem to enjoy themselves even while carrying locks as heavy as their bike frames and stopping for lights every two blocks. The rewards are seeing the urban fabric at a range close enough to explore crooked streets, read historical markers, and discover neighborhood haunts.

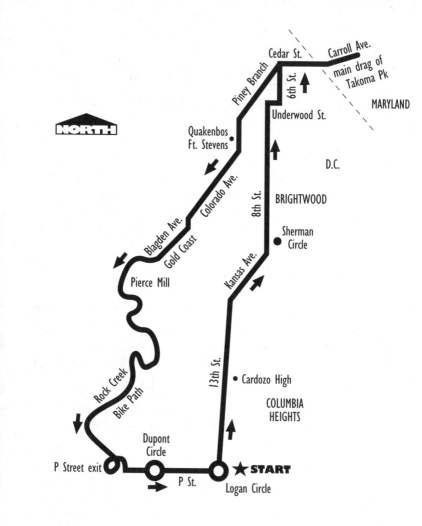

NORTH

Carroll Ave.
main drag of Takoma Pk
Cedar St.
MARYLAND
Piney Branch
6th St.
Underwood St.
Quakenbos
Ft. Stevens
D.C.
Colorado Ave.
8th St.
BRIGHTWOOD
Blagden Ave.
Gold Coast
Sherman Circle
Pierce Mill
Kansas Ave.
Rock Creek
Bike Path
13th St.
Cardozo High
COLUMBIA HEIGHTS
Dupont Circle
P Street exit
P St.
Logan Circle
★ **START**

HOW to get there

From Dupont Circle Metro, take Dupont Circle exit and cross the circle to P Street heading east. Ride six blocks to Logan Circle. From downtown, take Thirteenth Street north from Pennsylvania Avenue. From Capitol Hill, take Massachusetts Avenue west to Thirteenth Street and turn right.

DIREC-TIONS
for the ride

- Start at Logan Circle at the intersection of Vermont and Rhode Island avenues and Thirteenth Street N.W.
- Head north about twenty-five blocks (2.5 miles) on Thirteenth Street, a designated bike route.
- Watch for sign pointing to alternate bike route to Takoma Park. Soft right on Kansas Avenue.
- Left at Eighth Street to enter Brightwood neighborhood.
- In about twenty blocks, right on Underwood Street.
- In three blocks, left on Sixth Street N.W.
- Ride five blocks to Cedar Street N.W. To visit Takoma Park, Maryland, turn right on Cedar, which turns into Carroll Avenue (main street) after crossing under railroad tracks. To return to downtown D.C., turn left on Cedar and left on Piney Branch Road.
- Piney Branch to Fort Stevens (at left near Quackenbos Street).
- Continue on Piney Branch to Colorado Avenue (signed bike route). Turn right.
- Left at Seventeenth Street.
- In two short blocks, right on Blagden Avenue.
- Take Blagden Avenue to Beach Drive in Rock Creek Park.
- Turn right on Beach Drive.
- Left on Broad Branch.
- Immediate left through small parking lot to Pierce Mill.
- At Pierce Mill, join Rock Creek bike path heading south.
- In about 3 miles, take parkway exit marked for Dupont Circle.
- At top of exit ramp, right on P Street.
- Left on Twentieth Street to reach Dupont Circle Metro station (bike racks available).

Some people will never know these pleasures. Cowed by traffic and poor road maintenance, they stick to bike paths and country lanes. Basically, they're exhibiting good common sense, but I still think they're missing out. Try this ride on a Sunday morning, when traffic is at a minimum. Remember to bring along extra tubes, coins for pay phones, and, ideally, a buddy for this and other urban rides described in this book.

Start at historic Logan Circle, named for the Civil War general John A. Logan. The Civil War was the neighborhood's heyday. Gilded Age Washingtonians built preposterously large Victorian houses featuring turrets, finials, widow's walks, and any other architectural doodads they could think of. The remarkable thing is that the circle and its surrounding blocks have remained intact, even thrived with renovation in recent years. The circle itself was recently restored when two extra traffic lanes were removed in favor of grass and shrubs.

Follow bike-route signs up the beginning of the steep hill that is Thirteenth Street. You're in the midst of another architecturally interesting, but fairly gritty, neighborhood (Columbia Heights), so be careful. At the heights pass the magnificent edifice of Cardozo High, home to a famous marching band, and keep your eyes peeled for a bike-route sign pointing to Takoma Park via Third Street.

The scene remains urban but loses some of its grit in favor of green, for the houses of the Brightwood area are carefully tended and are surrounded by small lawns, azaleas, and evergreens. A former farming community that was developed with row houses in the early twentieth century, it's the type of place where people set up a transistor radio on the front porch to listen to a ball game while cutting the grass with an old push mower.

The ride heads due north across short hills on straight, quiet streets. Near the apex of the city of Washington, take a short detour to the area's first real suburb, Takoma Park, Maryland. Built after 1883 to provide inexpensive housing connected to the city by rail and streetcar, Takoma Park today is an amalgamation of many things: grand Queen Anne houses and tiny bungalows; tie-dyed types who never stopped being hippies and young lawyers; and quiet suburban living and city amenities. A good reason to stop here is the food. On Sundays a farmers' market fills part of Carroll Avenue, and there are good cafes and bakeries nearby as well. For now, at least, Takoma Park is also a suburb without malls. In 1995, development plans that would change that distinction began to make headway with the local government. Brick-lined Carroll Avenue is a real Main Street, complete with a clocktower and a pharmacy run by a gentleman everyone calls "Doc."

On the way back into town, stop at reconstructed Fort Stevens to peer over the same battlements where President Lincoln nervously watched the troops of Confederate General Jubal Early advance on the underdefended capital in 1864. Bullets whizzed by Abe's stovepipe hat until Lt. Colonel Oliver Wendell Holmes supposedly barked, "Get down, you fool!" Early was soon repelled, however. Today the site is mostly grass, but a little imagination reconstructs the scene.

Though heading south toward the city center, you will soon leave urbanized areas behind. Colorado and Blagden avenues cut diagonally across the street grid through the Gold Coast, a wealthy neighborhood with large Tudor houses. You will be coasting here, as the grades are all downhill. Soon you will arrive via Carton Barron Amphitheatre at Pierce Mill in Rock Creek Park. Take the Rock Creek Park bike path south and exit at Dupont Circle, the most cosmopolitan neighborhood in Washington. There are dozens of embassies, historic houses, movie theaters, art galleries, and bookshops in this historic district. After exploring the area on foot, you can either ride the six blocks east back to Logan Circle or jump on Metrorail's Red Line to go anywhere at all.

Dupont–Georgetown– Cleveland Park Loop

Distance:	7-mile loop
Approximate pedaling time:	2 hours
Terrain:	Hilly
Surface:	City roads
Things to see:	Phillips Gallery, Washington Cathedral, four historic districts, Embassy Row

If you could only block out the traffic, this would be the city ride that would make you forget you're in the city, for these are both Washington's leafiest and most affluent neighborhoods, each with its own character. Georgetown, which existed as a thriving port long before the District of Columbia was conceived, has its brick sidewalks, cobblestone streets, and absurdly narrow row houses; Dupont Circle its bistro and bookstore nightlife; Cleveland Park its rambling wooden houses and big shade trees; and Embassy Row its mansions that could have been plucked from Gatsby's North Shore. A stop along the way, the National Cathedral, features rolling grounds punctuated by flowering trees, and an herb garden that would be the envy of its English progenitors.

The ride should be taken at a very slow pace to enjoy views of gardens and stop to read plaques. Start at the Q Street entrance to the Dupont Circle Metro. The neighborhood's nerve center across the street is Kramer Books & Afterwords Cafe, which serves up spinach quiche with its Spinoza. After fortifying body and mind, head for P Street, a lively corridor of restaurants and bookshops. It's hard to believe that before 1873 this urbane row was a humble creek surrounded by farmland. Within thirty years this was the most fashionable address in Washington, by 1950 a slum, and now again pricey and restored.

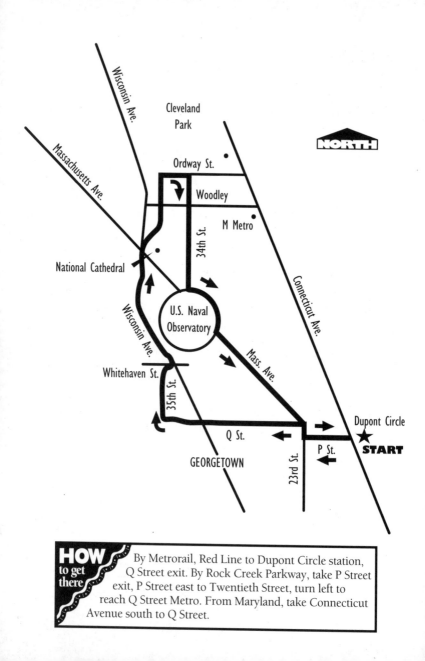

HOW to get there By Metrorail, Red Line to Dupont Circle station, Q Street exit. By Rock Creek Parkway, take P Street exit, P Street east to Twentieth Street, turn left to reach Q Street Metro. From Maryland, take Connecticut Avenue south to Q Street.

DIREC-TIONS for the ride

- From Q Street entrance to Dupont Circle Metro, head south on Twentieth Street two blocks to P Street. Turn right.
- In three blocks, right on Twenty-third Street and immediately left on Q Street.
- Cross Wisconsin Avenue in Georgetown; jog right and then left on Q Street again.
- Right on Thirty-fifth Street.
- Right on Whitehaven Street.
- Left on Wisconsin Avenue (heavy traffic for 10 blocks).
- Right through arched entrance to National Cathedral grounds.
- Exit Cathedral grounds and turn right on Woodley Road.
- Left on Thirty-sixth Street in Cleveland Park.
- In five blocks, right on Ordway Street.
- In two blocks, right on Thirty-fourth Street (heavy traffic).
- In about seven blocks, left on Massachusetts Avenue (bike route on sidewalk).
- Stay on sidewalk to Sheridan Circle at Twenty-third Street.
- Go around circle to stay on Massachusetts. In two blocks, left on Q Street.
- Return to Dupont Circle Metro.

Cross the 1914 Buffalo Bridge to Q Street for an introduction to some of Georgetown's finer houses. Farther up Q Street is Dumbarton Oaks, a palatial estate owned by Harvard University and open to the public for limited hours. Its attractions include a fantastic formal garden and a museum (designed by Philip Johnson) of pre-Columbian art. Cross Wisconsin Avenue, one of Washington's busiest shopping streets, and ride through more blocks of ornate old houses until Q Street ends.

After pedaling uphill and fighting Wisconsin Avenue traffic, you arrive some 400 feet above the level of the Potomac. The climb will be rewarded by a visit to one of the world's largest churches, the Washington Cathedral (National Cathedral). From some angles on

the Potomac's south bank, the limestone towers of this Gothic wonder actually loom over the Capitol dome. The cathedral was undertaken in 1907 using medieval construction methods and was just recently completed. There are some modern details, such as stained-glass windows commemorating the moon landing, and a gargoyle that parodies a modern lawyer on the run. There's an observation deck in one of three towers, a gift shop, a brass-rubbing center, and a small commercial greenhouse.

The cathedral borders Cleveland Park, Washington's newest historic district and unofficial Volvo capital of the free world. Its residents tend to be former free spirits now plugging through the upper echelons of journalism and law. The oldest house here dates from 1780. According to historian Kathleen Sinclair Wood, the area's frame houses and wraparound porches are "reminiscent of small-town America . . . within minutes of central Washington."

Exit Cleveland Park via busy Thirty-fourth Street to Massachusetts Avenue. As you turn left, the vice-president's residence, a white turreted structure on the grounds of the U.S. Naval Observatory, is visible beyond a fence on the right. (Careful: The intersection sees more bike accidents than any other in the city.) Straight ahead is the Naval Observatory itself, with its 120-year-old telescope, which was used to discover the moons of Mars in 1877, and the Master Clock of the United States, the world's most accurate timepiece.

The scenery gets much more grandiose as you head down Massachusetts Avenue. You pass the embassies of Britain, Brazil, Japan, and Turkey. There are formal gardens, specimen trees, and a statue of Winston Churchill flashing V-for-victory. The latest addition to this diplomatic corridor is a memorial to poet-philosopher Kahlil Gibran. Though lined by stately linden trees, this is not the most inspiring bicycling territory—you ride on a sidewalk on a street clogged with traffic—but it is a fitting end to a tour of Washington at its most cultivated.

ENTERING

PRINCE WILLIAM FOREST PARK

UNITED STATES DEPARTMENT OF THE INTERIOR
NATIONAL PARK SERVICE

Prince William Forest Park

Distance:	13-mile loop
Approximate pedaling time:	1 hour
Terrain:	Hilly
Surface:	Well-maintained park roads with no shoulder but little traffic
Things to see:	Reclaimed woodlands
Facilities:	Camping (RVs and tents) with hot showers, picnic grounds, rest rooms
Option:	Mountain biking

This is a simple, 13-mile ride that's great for getting into shape for longer rides. It includes a 6-mile loop you can ride a few times for a longer workout. You can even switch modes by bringing mountain bikes to ride the 20 miles of fire roads through the dense forest of this unusual National Park.

A few of the fire roads are closed to bikes. Check with the ranger before revving up the stump-jumper. He or she will give you a map showing approved routes. When this was written, routes *not* recommended for biking included the North Orenda Road and Old Pyrite Road. A park spokesperson also warned bikers against riding on the 35 miles of hiking trails. "Our rangers are ready to nab 'em," she said.

There's excellent camping (both tents and trailer hook-ups) should you wish to stay over to spend a second day hiking. Large groups can stay in one of five rustic camps ($165 for up to 200 campers) built by the Civilian Conservation Corps (CCC) in the 1930s. The young construction workers milled their wood on site from fallen trees. They were paid $1 a day. With unemployment near 25 percent nationally, there were plenty of takers. They also built

NORTH

Scenic Drive

Prince William
Forest Park

Quantico
Marine Base

619

95

Pine Grove Pinic Area
Parking

START

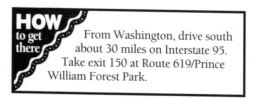

HOW
to get
there

From Washington, drive south
about 30 miles on Interstate 95.
Take exit 150 at Route 619/Prince
William Forest Park.

DIREC-TIONS for the ride

- From Pine Grove Picnic area, just off Route 619, ride north toward Carter Day Camp.
- Right on Scenic Drive.
- Continue counterclockwise on Scenic Drive. Camping available about halfway through the loop.
- At about mile 9, turn right to head toward park exit.
- Left into Pine Grove Picnic Area.

---

lakes near each site. Today these rough-hewn cabins, surrounded by forest and built of shingle, iron, and stone, are listed in the National Register of Historic Places.

Originally named Chopawamsic ("by the separation of the outlet"), the 16,000-acre park is a great place to relive history or to study natural history. Even cyclists may spot a wild turkey or white-tailed deer, or wend along the edge of a meadow or a stand of Virginia pine.

The park is also an example of environmental restoration. When founded by Scotsmen in the 1700s, this area was second only to New York among New World ports. By the next century pyrite mining had become the area's economic base. Sulphur was extracted from this fool's gold and refined for industrial uses. But by 1933 the centuries of mining and farming had exhausted the land. Siltation clogged Quantico Creek and consigned Dumfries Harbor to oblivion. The federal government bought 17,000 acres and ultimately directed that it be rehabilitated as wilderness. The CCC was assigned to the job, and the labor was imported from tent camps right in Washington. In 1948 Prince William Forest Park was born with another social purpose: to provide inner-city youth with camping facilities. The park still serves that function.

Where once were barren fields are now eighty-nine species of shrubs and trees, including hickory, beech, and mountain laurel. Bisected by many streams and paths, the park looks like a piece of nature preserved in its pristine state. The new-growth forest is home to beaver, red fox, copperhead snakes, and the occasional bald eagle. But there are also remnants of civilization: foundations, orchards, cemeteries, and remains of the old pyrite mine.

The park's function of harboring Prince William County's open space becomes increasingly important as development fans out from Washington with accelerating speed. Right now, the park offers one of the few on-road rides in this book where I can guarantee light traffic and uncluttered scenery. There is a small price to pay: This ride requires an admission pass. A one-week ticket costs $3 per carload; leave the guzzler home and the price is $1 per biker or hiker.

Park officials are experimenting with planting grasses to filter runoff pollution that now seeps into the creeks. They hope that these watercourses will supply potable water in just a few years. If so, hot cyclists will probably be among the first to dunk their heads and drink deeply.

20 Prince George's Urban Farmland

Distance:	17-mile loop
Approximate pedaling time:	2 hours
Terrain:	Rolling
Surface:	Country roads
Things to see:	Rustic farm buildings, fields, ponds, and creeks
Option:	Trip to Goddard Space Flight Center

Just like Prince William Forest Park, the Beltsville Agricultural Research Center provides an oasis of green in a rapidly urbanizing area. Whereas the park offers a pristine look at acres of woodlands, the research center preserves another vanishing landscape: that of the American farm.

As the center says in its own brochure, "From the air, the center looks like a 9-mile-long, 4-mile-wide quilted blanket of green fields, pastures, and orchards." All of this can be found only 15 miles northeast of the city. Along with the quiet roads, this makes the center a favorite both for bike racers in training and day-trippers coming from the neighboring University of Maryland.

Located on 7,500 acres in Prince George's County, Maryland, the center was created in 1910 to study better means of soil conservation and animal husbandry. Its nucleus was a 475-acre farm acquired by the federal government at that time. Among the notable results of research conducted here are the plump-breasted Thanksgiving turkey (the one the pilgrims ate was a stringy wild turkey), the "modern hog" (it's leaner and longer than the old-fashioned pig and has an extra vertebra for more chops), the Atlantic potato (good for low-fat chips), and the domestic strawberry. Today, the research center is de-

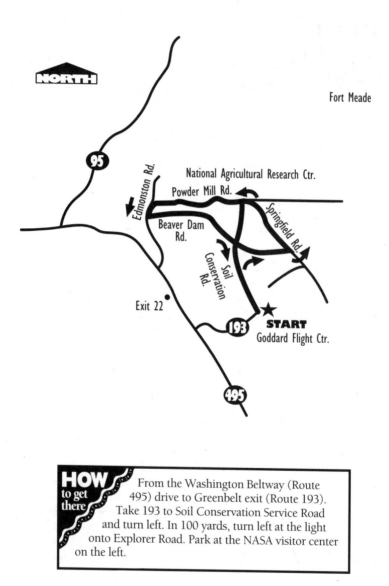

NORTH

Fort Meade

National Agricultural Research Ctr.

Powder Mill Rd.

Edmonston Rd.

Springfield Rd.

Beaver Dam Rd.

Soil Conservation Rd.

Exit 22

193 START
Goddard Flight Ctr.

495

HOW to get there
From the Washington Beltway (Route 495) drive to Greenbelt exit (Route 193). Take 193 to Soil Conservation Service Road and turn left. In 100 yards, turn left at the light onto Explorer Road. Park at the NASA visitor center on the left.

DIREC-TIONS for the ride

- From the parking lot at the NASA visitor center, ride back to the traffic light at Soil Conservation Road (SCS Road), and turn left.
- Head north on SCS Road to Beaver Dam Road; turn right.
- Sharp left on Springfield Road.
- Left on Powder Mill Road. Pass turn-off for Soil COnsevation Road on left.
- Look for driveway to log-cabin visitors center on left.
- Left on Edmonston Road.
- In about 0.5 mile, left on Beaver Dam Road.
- Right on SCS Road to return to start.

voted primarily to studies of the environment and global food supplies. It is operated by the U.S. Department of Agriculture, which maintains on the grounds more than 1,000 buildings and thousands of cattle, turkeys, and chickens.

Many of those buildings are of the rustic variety: great wooden silos, rambling, weathered barns, and clapboard farmhouses with sagging front porches. What it amounts to (for the cyclist, at least) is a wide-open space in a region where that's rare. The roads are well-paved. Some have broad, clean shoulders, while others are somewhat narrow.

Particularly when traffic is light early in the morning, the ride is a delight. The loop described in this ride is only a sample—there are other quiet lanes to explore as well. You'll pass ponds, stands of hardwood, pastures full of cows and sheep, a strawberry patch, orchards, old railroad tracks, and two creeks.

The center once looked inward and did not encourage public visitation, but it recently put on a bright new face that encourages both recreation and education. For example, in 1989 the center dedicated a new visitors center in a restored log cabin, originally modeled after

the lodges in Yellowstone National Park. The so-called Log Lodge was built from 1934 to 1937 by the Civilian Conservation Corps (CCC) from timbers 40 to 50 feet long, harvested and milled on site. The CCC also built the major roads through the facility. Until 1985 the lodge was used as a cafeteria, where diners included Dwight D. Eisenhower and Nikita Khrushchev. It stands on Powder Mill Road on the western portion of this route. The restoration cost more than $500,000. Go in to get a map and see the exhibits.

On the way in or out, you can visit the visitors center at the Goddard Space Flight Center, a NASA research facility with a $1 billion annual budget and 12,000 employees. The museum at the center offers film clips in an eight-screen cinema, a solar telescope for sunspot viewing, an outdoor rocket park, and a simulated space-flight trainer. It's open daily 10:00 A.M. to 4:00 P.M. The center also hosts model-rocket launches two Sunday afternoons a month. Admission is free. Call (301) 286–8981 for more information.

Two Creeks of Maryland

Distance:	13 miles, one way
Approximate pedaling time:	3 hours
Terrain:	Flat
Surface:	Paved off-road trails and shoulder of parkway
Things to see:	Historic mill, woodlands, suburban neighborhoods
Facilities:	Rest rooms, playgrounds

When it comes to development of off-road multi-use trails, Prince George's and eastern Montgomery counties in Maryland are quickly catching up with their neighbors. This ride connects two off-road trails along Sligo Creek Parkway and the Northwest Branch of the Anacostia River, each traversing bucolic parks. They are particularly worth exploring if you live in the area and bicycle with a young family. The quiet, 5-mile-long Northwest Branch is a good venue to graduate youngsters from training wheels.

The ride starts at Montgomery County's Wheaton Regional Park, just 6 miles north of Washington. Look around a bit before you leave. On 496 acres, the park includes a hockey-size, open-air ice rink (I've even cycled to my skating sessions in winter), Brookside Gardens (second only to the National Arboretum in its seasonal floral display), a miniature railway with a brand-new station house, and a merry-go-round..

The off-road trail heads south through quiet suburban neighborhoods and along Sligo Creek Park, which is roughly akin to Rock Creek Park for this area of Maryland. In a few miles the trail is supplanted by an on-road route on the narrow shoulder of Sligo Creek

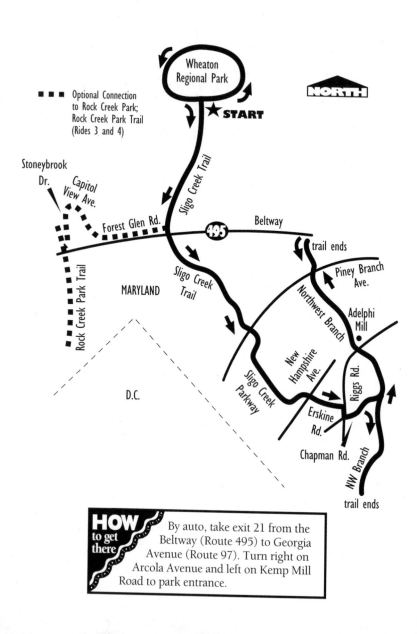

Wheaton Regional Park

★ START

NORTH

Optional Connection to Rock Creek Park; Rock Creek Park Trail (Rides 3 and 4)

Stoneybrook Dr.

Capitol View Ave.

Forest Glen Rd.

Beltway 495

trail ends

Rock Creek Park Trail

Sligo Creek Trail

Sligo Creek Trail

MARYLAND

Piney Branch Ave.

Northwest Branch

Adelphi Mill

D.C.

Sligo Creek Parkway

New Hampshire Ave.

Riggs Rd.

Erskine Rd.

Chapman Rd.

NW Branch

trail ends

HOW to get there — By auto, take exit 21 from the Beltway (Route 495) to Georgia Avenue (Route 97). Turn right on Arcola Avenue and left on Kemp Mill Road to park entrance.

- Start at Wheaton Regional Park, Orebaugh and Arcola avenues, Wheaton, Maryland. Ride the loop road around the park.
- Ride south on Sligo hiker/biker trail (off road).
- At Piney Branch Road, off-road path ends. Ride on shoulder of Sligo Creek Parkway.
- Sligo Creek Parkway ends at New Hampshire Avenue. Turn left on New Hampshire and immediately right on Erskine Street.
- Right on Riggs Road (busy).
- Left on Chapman Road.
- Right on Northwest Branch hiker/biker trail (off-road).
- At end of park, turn around and double back.
- Cross Riggs Road to reach historic Adelphi Mill and continue to northern end of park.

Option: Connection to Rock Creek Park in Maryland (2 miles).
- Head south from Wheaton Regional Park as stated above.
- Just before passing under Beltway bridge, turn right on Forest Glen Road.
- At intersection of Seminary Road, turn right on Capitol View Avenue.
- Capitol View becomes Stoneybrook, which ends at Beach Drive (Rock Creek Park).

Option: While on Stoneybrook, turn right into visitors center for Mormon Temple (see Ride 4).

Parkway, a two-lane road that winds through some pretty Takoma Park neighborhoods. The motorists are used to seeing cyclists, but take extra care to be safe and visible nonetheless. The shoulder is quite narrow, if not nonexistent. A mile of the parkway between Maple Avenue and Piney Branch Road is closed to motor vehicles every Sunday, 11:00 A.M. –6:00 P.M.

The parkway ends at New Hampshire Avenue. From here an on-road route through neighborhoods will connect you to the restored

Adelphi Mill, built in 1790 by two brothers from Pennsylvania (hence "Adelphi"), abandoned in 1850, and restored (albeit not to working condition) in the 1950s. One of the only two surviving grist mills in Prince George's County, it's used today for weddings and meetings.

The mill is located midway through a 5-mile stretch of off-road trail parallel to the Northwest Branch. This tributary of the Anacostia River is well stocked with trout by the U.S. Fish and Wildlife Service. Located just steps away is the miller's cottage, built of fieldstone in 1792 and now leased as a private residence for the county archaeologist.

The ravine is deep and wild-looking, but the path is flat and quiet. There are some mica-covered boulders in the stream, a duck pond, and a portion of streambed full of submerged carbonized logs. These soggy hunks of driftwood are estimated to be more than 120 million years old. If removed from their aquatic state, they would disintegrate.

Like Sligo Creek, this oblong park straddles Prince George's and Montgomery counties.

Around Avenel
A Piece of Potomac

Distance:	12 miles
Approximate pedaling time:	1 hour
Terrain:	Rolling
Surface:	Smooth roads, some with adjacent off-road trails
Things to see:	Stream-cut ravines, meadows, ritzy neighborhoods
Facilities:	PGA golf course, Potomac Village shopping area with food, banks, boutiques

Far from my tie-dyed, gritty town of Takoma Park ("where old hippies go to die") lies a land of horse farms and houses the size of small hotels, five-car garages and home squash courts. It's Potomac, Maryland, the Washington area's own East Egg, and it's threaded with some two-lane blacktop that beckons cyclists. This chapter outlines a figure eight that's a great training ride.

A bit of background. Until 1880, Potomac was called Offutt's Crossroads, named for the area's largest landowners. It remained sleepy and rural until the early part of the century, when some fields were turned into estates. Additional cachet came with the 1924 opening of the Congressional Country Club, followed by the 1930 founding of the Potomac Hunt Club: a squirearchy was born. Potomac residents today are more likely to go golfing or shopping than fox hunting, but the area has retained many horse pastures and bridle paths. Equestrian fever still runs high.

Start at Avenel, a 1,000-acre former horse farm that is now a luxury housing development centered around a new 225-acre, professional-

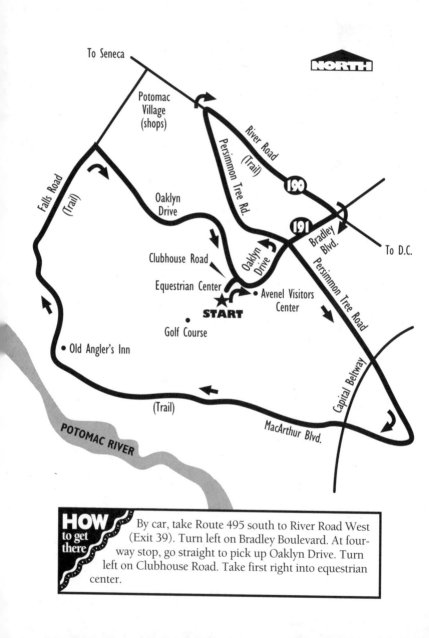

To Seneca

NORTH

Potomac Village (shops)

River Road

Persimmon Tree Rd. (Trail)

190

191

Bradley Blvd.

To D.C.

Falls Road (Trail)

Oaklyn Drive

Oaklyn Drive

Clubhouse Road

Equestrian Center

Avenel Visitors Center

START

Persimmon Tree Road

Golf Course

Old Angler's Inn

Capital Beltway

(Trail)

MacArthur Blvd.

POTOMAC RIVER

HOW to get there By car, take Route 495 south to River Road West (Exit 39). Turn left on Bradley Boulevard. At four-way stop, go straight to pick up Oaklyn Drive. Turn left on Clubhouse Road. Take first right into equestrian center.

DIRECTIONS for the ride

- Leave equestrian center via driveway.
- Left on Clubhouse Road.
- At T intersection, right on Oaklyn Drive.
- At 4-way stop, left on Persimmon Tree Road.
- At oblique T intersection, right on River Road (Route 190).
- At 4-way intersection with traffic light, right on Bradley Boulevard (Route 191).
- At 4-way stop, left on Persimmon Tree Road.
- At T intersection at bottom of hill, right on MacArthur Boulevard.
- Right on Falls Road.
- Right on Oaklyn Drive.
- Right on Clubhouse Road.
- Right into equestrian center.

circuit golf course. Avenel is packed with visual niceties and amenities: meadows, rows of freshly planted trees, iron lampposts, preserved forests. Even the brass-plated, neo-everything architecture isn't bad by local standards.

Begin in the gravel parking area of the equestrian center, where pastures engulf a fine old timber-frame horse barn. After heading down a short drive, take a right if you want to see the Tournament Players Club, where as many as 32,000 people convene each May to watch the Kemper Open golf tournament. Otherwise, turn left on Clubhouse Road to start the ride.

A right on Oaklyn Drive takes you past the information center (they were nice to me despite my gritty bike clothes), where you can get the scoop on million-dollar homes in eight separate Avenel developments. The pool-table-smooth road provides entertaining dips and turns, and the scenery is impeccably groomed. Even the meadows of goldenrod and second-growth forests look picked over and arranged. The housing cluster on the right is called Player's Crossing; on the left is Player's Gate. (The developer calls these villages, but if they are, I'm Greg LeMond.)

Turn left on Persimmon Tree Drive and leave Avenel for an older neighborhood of grand ranch houses and Tudors mixed in with new "tract mansions," as Henry Allen of the *Washington Post* dubs Potomac's large new houses. The road surface remains superb. Persimmon Tree winds a bit until you come to a busy, oblique intersection with River Road. Be careful of heavy traffic here. Turn right to stay on this route; turn left if you need refreshments in the Potomac Village shopping area, less than one-eighth of a mile down River Road. I recommend the Mrs. Fields Cookies (sandwiches and breakfast also available) and the bookshop next door.

Back on the route, follow River Road east for about 1.5 miles. This is a busy, two-lane arterial, but there's a parallel path for bailing out if you feel uncomfortable in traffic. It's a straight shot past more big homes until you turn right at a traffic light on Bradley Boulevard.

Bradley is more lightly traveled, but there is also an adjacent path available, smooth, albeit narrow. Proceed to a four-way stop at the intersection with Persimmon Tree. Take a left (this is the knot in the figure-eight) to explore a new part of Persimmon Tree. You pass another part of Avenel ("Willowgate"), cross the Capital Beltway on an overpass, and descend to the bluffs of the Potomac River. Now heading west on MacArthur Boulevard, you're riding through a neighborhood mixing older bungalows with newer homes and dense vegetation. On the left you'll pass the Naval Surface Warfare Center, which is a research facility, not a dock or shipyard. What looks like a mile-long Quonset hut is used for testing model ships. Just over the horizon find the Carderock Recreation Area (a mecca for rock-climbers and rappellers), rapids of the Potomac, and islands named Offutt, Turkey, Vaso, Hermit, and Perry.

MacArthur Boulevard is popular for serious cyclists in training. To its credit, Montgomery County has alerted drivers with recently posted "Share the Road" signs. There's also an adjacent off-road trail/shoulder. I'd rather ride the road; stick to the shoulder if you prefer a 10-mph pace, cars bother you, or you're riding with children.

At Old Angler's Inn, follow the road to the right as it begins a mile-long climb through dense woods. There's a nice, wide shoulder along this stretch. The next turn is a right onto Falls Road. You have the option of turning left and descending into Great Falls Park, where you can pick up the C & O Canal trail and ride a dozen miles back to Washington. If you're staying with the route, be alert, as Falls Road is narrow and crowded. Again, an adjacent trail on the left offers a way out. A right turn on Oaklyn Drive brings you through more of Avenel ("Oaklyn Woods," "Chartwell") through open space set aside for the future water-treatment plant, and back to Clubhouse Drive, where you can return to the equestrian center's parking area.

To Edwards Ferry

Distance:	10-mile loop
Approximate pedaling time:	1 hour
Terrain:	One third flat, two thirds hilly
Surface:	Smooth two-lane roads and dirt towpath
Things to see:	Ruins at Edwards Ferry, farm country, wildlife area, swamp, C & O Canal
Facilities:	Camping

This loop explores the Potomac's scenic bottomlands, where a slower, straighter part of the river above Great Falls glides by cornfields, swamps, sod farms, oak forest, and ruins. It's a good ride to append to Ride 24 (Sugarland Loop) or Ride 25 (Escape to the Maryland Countryside), but it also stands well on its own.

Start about 15 miles west of D.C. at the Sycamore Landing parking area of the C & O Canal. This is the land of Seneca sandstone, the building material for the Smithsonian castle and other Washington landmarks. Sycamore Landing is an old canal landing abandoned in 1924 with the rest of the C & O. The canal is dry here and a hardwood forest is overtaking its bed. You can look over the Potomac to Maddox Island.

Ride away from the canal through McKee-Beshers Wildlife Area, which looks like a farm because its lowland fields are sown with corn and other plants that attract wildlife. The wildlife attract hunters, so expect gunfire in hunting season. Cross Horsepen Branch on a bridge and turn left on River Road, which becomes Old River Road when it narrows suddenly to one lane and enters the woods. (This was an Indian path later used to roll hogsheads of tobacco to Georgetown.)

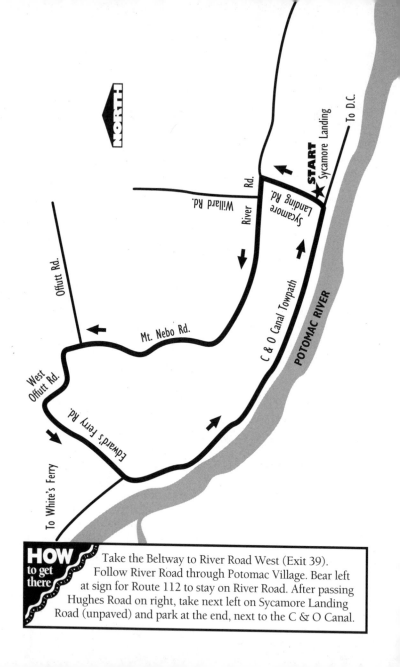

NORTH

To D.C.

Sycamore Landing

START

Sycamore Landing Rd.

River Rd.

Willard Rd.

Offutt Rd.

Mt. Nebo Rd.

West Offutt Rd.

C & O Canal Towpath

POTOMAC RIVER

Edward's Ferry Rd.

To White's Ferry

HOW to get there — Take the Beltway to River Road West (Exit 39). Follow River Road through Potomac Village. Bear left at sign for Route 112 to stay on River Road. After passing Hughes Road on right, take next left on Sycamore Landing Road (unpaved) and park at the end, next to the C & O Canal.

DIRECTIONS for the ride

- North (away from canal) on Sycamore Landing Road (unpaved).
- Left on River Road.
- Bear right on Mt. Nebo Road.
- Left on Offutt Road.
- Left on West Offutt Road.
- Left on Edwards Ferry Road.
- Left on C & O Canal towpath.
- Return to Sycamore Landing.

There's a grade to climb here with a view of a hardwood swamp on the left. I've seen red-tailed hawks perched on the snags of dead sycamores. Be looking for bits of prickly pear clinging to rock outcrops on the right. The cactus is native to the East.

Past a shale rock face, pass through a mile-long lawn—a sod farm. The scenery becomes vaguely British when hedgerows appear, but less so where large homes on five-acre lots have replaced eroded farmland. Several large horse farms and Montgomery County's enlightened rural preservation program have helped save a semblance of countryside. Glide down Edwards Ferry Road past fields once strewn with cobblestones and boulders (this was the prehistoric Potomac's bed when the river was much higher). There are still some rocks in these piedmont fields.

At Edwards Ferry, there's a well-preserved lock house and the stone-and-brick ruins of a grain warehouse. The ferry landing was once a transfer point for wagonloads of grain, coal, and supplies. Across this wide, fairly calm part of the Potomac is Virginia's Goose Creek.

Pick up the towpath for a 3-mile return to Sycamore Landing. The towpath can get pretty muddy along this stretch, but it's not so bad that you would need a mountain bike. There's camping on the canal at Chisel Branch Hiker-Biker Camp (water pumps and outhouse available), but check ahead to see if you need reservations.

Sugarland Loop

Distance:	10 miles
Approximate pedaling time:	1 hour
Terrain:	Rolling
Surface:	Well-paved country roads
Things to see:	Old C & O Canal aqueduct, Homestead Farm (for pick-your-own fruit in season)

Here's the sweetest ride in Montgomery Country—a little corner of road cycling heaven within forty-five minutes of downtown Washington. The Sugarland Loop lies in the county's northwest corner, long a favorite destination for area cyclists. You'll be likely to run into group rides organized by the Potomac Pedalers club or training rides organized by any of the several local racing clubs.

The Sugarland Loop is a perfect 10-mile jaunt. For a longer ride, combine it with Ride 24 (To Edward's Ferry), using River Road as a connector. For a *really* long ride, try Ride 25 (Escape to the Maryland Countryside), which covers some of the same roads.

Start at Riley's Lock, off River Road just west of Seneca Road. The parking lot here provides a convenient staging area not only for cyclists but also for hikers heading out on the C & O Canal towpath, for picnickers using the grassy park on the river, and for boaters putting in at Seneca Creek for easy access to the Potomac. Be sure to take a look at the aqueduct, which used to carry the canal *over* Seneca Creek on its way west. Its huge blocks of Seneca sandstone still arch over the wide creek, but the canal dried up along here years ago.

Ride back toward River Road along Riley's Lock Road, which provides a nice creek-side warm-up. Then turn west onto River Road for

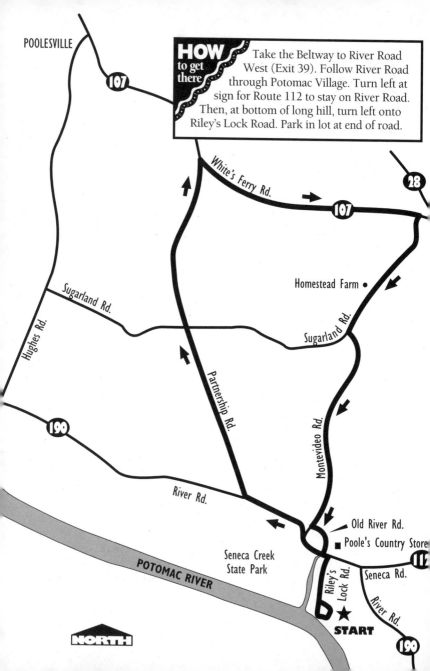

POOLESVILLE

107

HOW to get there
Take the Beltway to River Road West (Exit 39). Follow River Road through Potomac Village. Turn left at sign for Route 112 to stay on River Road. Then, at bottom of long hill, turn left onto Riley's Lock Road. Park in lot at end of road.

White's Ferry Rd.

28

107

Homestead Farm •

Sugarland Rd.

Hughes Rd.

Sugarland Rd.

Partnership Rd.

190

Montevideo Rd.

River Rd.

Old River Rd.

Poole's Country Store

112

Seneca Creek State Park

POTOMAC RIVER

Riley's Lock Rd.

Seneca Rd.

River Rd.

★ START

190

NORTH

DIRECTIONS for the ride

- From start/finish at Riley's Lock parking area, ride away from river on Riley's Lock Road.
- Left on River Road.
- Right on Partnership Road in about a mile.
- Follow Partnership Road to end, crossing Sugarland Road en route.
- Right on White's Ferry Road.
- Right on Sugarland Road at cluster of small houses. Ride carefully, as Sugarland narrows to a single lane of concrete slab roadway with dirt shoulders.
- Pass Homestead Farm, a favorite pick-your-own destination, on the right.
- Left on Montevideo Road.
- Left on Old River Road just before Montevideo ends at (new) River Road.
- Left on River Road at Poole's Country Store.
- Immediate right on Riley's Lock Road to return to parking area.

another mile, keeping an eye out for your right turn onto Partnership Road.

Partnership Road is a cyclist's dream road—few cars, lined by woods and horse farms, very few houses and driveways, just one intersection, just a couple of hills. Nothing could be simpler or nicer.

Then, make a sharp right onto White's Ferry Road. This is also a beautiful stretch of roadway, but more heavily traveled.

Turn right after a few miles onto Sugarland Road. You'll soon pass by Homestead Farm, which helps keep this area's agricultural tradition alive by offering pick-your-own fruits and vegetables from late May (strawberries) through October (pumpkins). If you'd like to sample the farm's offerings, make a quick detour up the driveway. The owners operate a small stand where you can buy already-picked produce.

Soon after Homestead Farm, turn left onto Montevideo Road. You'll dive down a short hill, cross a one-lane bridge, then climb up the other side on your way to another of this area's country institutions. Poole's Country Store, located on Old River Road toward the end of this ride, is a favorite all-purpose stop. You can refill your water bottle, buy a soda or cup of coffee, pick up a sandwich, catch up on the latest community news, or just sit on the front stoop and reflect on a perfect 10-mile ride.

For the Pros
Escape to the Maryland Countryside

Distance:	40- or 61-mile loop
Approximate pedaling time:	3 or 5 hours
Terrain:	Very hilly
Surface:	Suburban and country roads
Things to see:	Horse farms, fields, historic Poolesville, Maryland, Sugarloaf Mountain, Potomac riverfront
Options:	21-mile round-trip ride to Sugarloaf Mountain; end-of-ride return to Metrorail station

This is a route suggested by a person who knows more about biking than almost anyone around the Beltway: Mike Dornfield, a former associate bicycling coordinator for Washington, D.C.

Mike developed the route as a weekend getaway, but I've adapted it as a ride from Metrorail's Red Line through the inner suburbs of Montgomery County, with a destination of the quiet country town of Poolesville, a Civil War site of minor importance. On the way out and the way back you bisect the tony community of Potomac, Maryland, where the huge houses are likely to be augmented by a horse barn and a steeplechase course. The ride concludes with a historic section of the Potomac River before ending in Georgetown.

Start at Metrorail's Grosvenor Station. (This commencement point may also be reached by riding through Rock Creek Park, as described in Rides 3 and 4.) The immediate area is strictly suburban blah, with a six-lane road and ramps dominating the scenery. But a nifty suburban road called Tuckerman Lane will soon whisk you away from all that. Although not designated a bike route, Tuckerman was clearly designed for two wheelers. After starting off with four surprisingly

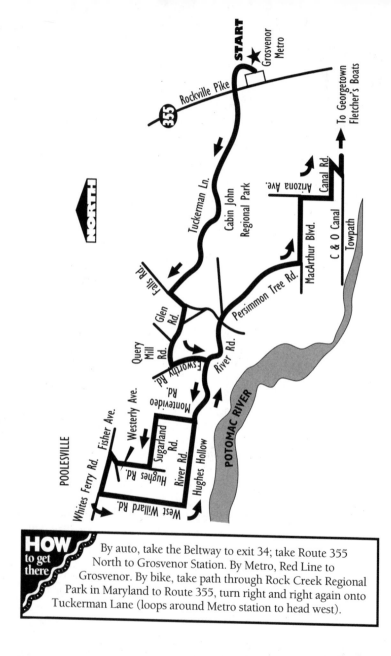

START

Grosvenor Metro

Rockville Pike

355

Tuckerman Ln.

Cabin John Regional Park

NORTH

Arizona Ave.

Canal Rd.

To Georgetown
Fletcher's Boats

MacArthur Blvd.

Persimmon Tree Rd.

C & O Canal
Towpath

Falls Rd.

Glen Rd.

Query Mill Rd.

Esworthy Rd.

River Rd.

POTOMAC RIVER

Montevideo Rd.

Westerly Ave.

Fisher Ave.

POOLESVILLE

Sugarland Rd.

Hughes Rd.

River Rd.

Hughes Hollow

Whites Ferry Rd.

West Willard Rd.

HOW to get there
By auto, take the Beltway to exit 34; take Route 355 North to Grosvenor Station. By Metro, Red Line to Grosvenor. By bike, take path through Rock Creek Regional Park in Maryland to Route 355, turn right and right again onto Tuckerman Lane (loops around Metro station to head west).

DIRECTIONS for the ride

- From Grosvenor station, Red Line of Metrorail, take east ramp out of station to Tuckerman Lane. Turn left to head west.
- Cross Route 355 (traffic light) to continue on Tuckerman.
- Take Tuckerman past camping area and Cabin John Regional Park.
- Left on Falls Road.
- First right on Glen Road. Stay on Glen for several miles.
- Bear left, downhill, onto Query Mill Road.
- After quick, brisk descent, turn right on Esworthy Road.
- At T intersection, left on Seneca Road (Route 112).
- Continue straight as Seneca Road merges with River Road.
- In several miles, right on Montevideo Road (just past Poole's Country Store, a good pit stop).
- At four-way intersection, left on Sugarland Road.
- At T intersection, right on Hughes Road.
- Take Hughes Road into town of Poolesville.
- Left on White's Ferry Road in Poolesville.
- Left on West Willard Road (near high school).
- After steep descent, left on River Road.
- Turn right with River Road as Seneca Road continues straight. (To avoid drastic hills and fast traffic on this next stretch of River Road, see "Return option" below.)
- Stay on River Road (use shoulder) through town of Potomac.
- After main intersection of town of Potomac, right on Persimmon Tree Road.
- In several miles (all downhill), left on MacArthur Boulevard. Return to Washington via Cabin John and Glen Echo.
- Back in Washington, right on Arizona Avenue N.W.
- Left on Canal Road near railroad bridge.
- Hard right at entrance to Fletcher's Boat House (canoe rental, refreshments, and fishing gear available).
- Take towpath of C & O Canal to Georgetown, where ride ends.

Mid-ride option (21-mile trip to Sugarloaf Mountain):

- In Poolesville, left on Fisher Avenue (Route 107).
- In 2 miles, right on Wasche Road.
- In 2.5 miles, right on Martinsburg Road, which becomes Dickerson Road.
- In Dickerson, right on Mount Ephraim Road; ride 2.5 miles, cross Comus Road, and enter Sugarloaf preserve.
- Backtrack via Mount Ephraim to Comus Road.
- Left on Comus Road.
- Right on Peach Tree Road.
- Left on Route 28 and immediately right on Cattail Road.
- Right on Fisher Avenue in Poolesville.

Return option: To avoid hilliest stretch of River Road, continue straight onto Seneca Road at point where River Road turns right past entrance to Bretton Woods Recreation Center. Retrace route along Esworthy, Query Mill, and Glen roads to Falls Road. Turn right on Falls Road, then left on River Road to continue ride to Georgetown. Or turn left on Falls Road and pick up Tuckerman Lane back to Grosvenor Metro.

---

quiet lanes going through an area of condominium apartments, it narrows to two lanes but with a shoulder wide enough for a fire truck.

The scenery is split levels and driveways as far as the eye can see, but traffic remains fairly light, and many of the yards are planted with azaleas and flowering trees. Soon you bisect the creek ravine that contains Cabin John Regional Park, which includes a petting zoo, a 1-mile minature railroad, and seven primitive campsites. At Falls Road, just past a nursery, you run into a row of small farmsteads with graceful old houses and barns, but don't be fooled—you're not in the country yet. Falls Road winds through the countrified estates of upper Potomac, where the squirearchy have maintained a semblance of the farmscape for horse pastures.

The real country kicks in just past 5,000-acre Seneca Creek State Park at the town of Seneca. From here you can traverse roads lined with wildflowers and high meadows overlooking the Potomac, then huff and puff uphill through real horse farms until reaching the town of Poolesville, which was contested during the Civil War. Founded in 1793 by the merchant John Poole, Poolesville has remained a country town despite some recent development. There's a twenty-building historict district and several antique shops worth visiting along its tree-lined streets.

The ride downhill from Poolesville has got to be one of the greatest delights in all of cycling. It's an almost vertical descent on a winding country road with pastures and creeks and woods and dancing figures of Queen Anne's lace creeping up to its edge. On the horizon you can sense the valley floor and the surging Potomac, while the foothills of the Blue Ridge Mountains rise into Virginia on the far side. It's a wonderful place to watch the sun set, framed by streaking clouds and golden grasses and grains.

Back on River Road, be prepared for more pretty scenery as you pass polo grounds, a wildlife management area, and a state park. After Riley's Lock Road, River Road turns right and subjects you to some drastic hills, and increasing traffic on the way through forests and then more estates of Potomac. Pass through Potomac's clogged center, then turn right on Persimmon Tree Drive to return to Washington via MacArthur Boulevard—a route described in Ride 11.

An optional return route avoids this last stretch of River Road *and* gives you the further option of returning to your starting point at the Grosvenor Metro. After passing Riley's Lock Road, simply continue straight on Seneca Road as River Road turns right. Retrace your route along Esworthy, Query Mill, Glen, Falls, and Tuckerman roads back to the Grosvenor station.

An optional ride from Poolesville takes you to the Washington area's only "mountain"—1,280-foot Sugarloaf Mountain, a National Historic Landmark surrounded by a 3,000-acre, privately owned preserve. Sugarloaf has been called "an outpost of the Appalachians." During the Civil War, Union troops used this precipice to observe General Robert E. Lee fording the Potomac at White's Ferry en route to Antietam Battlefield. Feeling really hardy? Ride to Sugarloaf's peak before turning back.

For the Pros
The Three-State Special

Distance:	62-mile loop
Approximate pedaling time:	6 hours
Terrain:	Hilly
Surface:	Back roads and two-laners with wide shoulders
Things to see:	Antietam Battlefield, Harpers Ferry National Historic Park, farmland

If all cyclists were like David Brown, books like this would never be published. Mr. Brown, a Washington lawyer, owns a weekend house in Round Hill, Virginia, 5 miles from the end of the W & OD trail. With a detailed Virginia map in hand, he started creating his own bike routes that include historic and scenic areas of Virginia, West Virginia, and Maryland. My great thanks to him for sharing his two favorites, which I've combined here into one long ride.

Many of the roads are quiet and little traveled. Just to the west is an apple-growing region. The busier routes feature wide shoulders. The two Potomac crossings can be made on safe bridges. By turning around at South Mountain Natural Area in Maryland, you can shave about one-fifth the distance from the ride.

The ride cuts a swath between the Blue Ridge and Short Hill mountains. It also takes you through the towns of Round Hill, Virginia; Sharpsburg, Maryland; Brunswick, Maryland; and Lovettsville, Virginia. Located in Washington County, Brunswick was once a thriving railroad town, with more than 1,300 people working for the B & O system. Much of its gritty heritage survives, along with a few trains carrying commuters to Washington. Its old houses are arranged in a cozy grid in the shadow of the Catoctin Mountains.

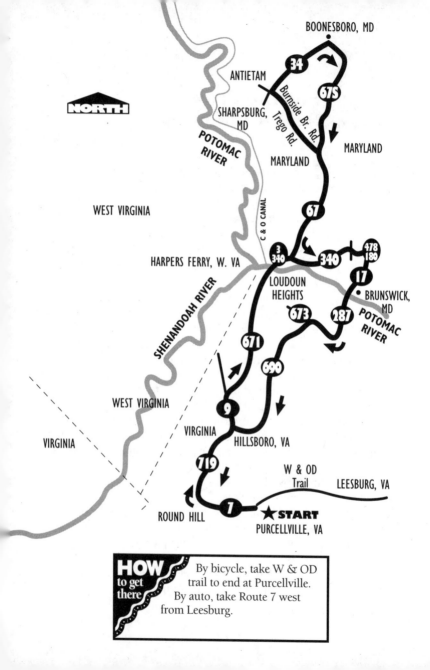

DIREC-TIONS for the ride

Note: Follow directions for Sharpsburg section carefully, as not every small street is shown on the map.

- From Twenty-first Street in Purcellville (end of W & OD trail), head west on old Route 7 through old community of Round Hill, Virginia.
- Right to head north on Route 719.
- Near town of Hillsboro, Route 719 comes to a T. Turn left on Route 9.
- Second right onto Route 671.
- Head north to Loudoun Heights, Virginia. Cross Potomac on bridge. Road merges with Route 340 in Maryland (four lanes with wide shoulders).

Optional trip to Harpers Ferry, West Virginia:

Left on 340 to historical park (about 2 miles). Double back to rejoin ride at Route 67.

- Left on Route 67.
- Pass by towns of Garretts Mill, August, Yarrowsburg, and Gapland, to South Mountain Natural Area.
- Left on Trego Road (becomes Mt. Briar Road).
- Left on Porterstown Road.
- At T intersection, left on Route 34 (busy).
- Ride through town of Sharpsburg; right on Route 65.
- Right off Route 65 to battlefield visitor center. **Option:** 7-mile tour of battlefield (details at visitors center).
- From visitors center, left on Route 65.
- Left on Route 34.
- Ride into town of Boonesboro. At traffic light, right on Alternate Route 40 East.
- Right on Route 67 south.
- Take Route 67 to Route 340. Turn left to head east.
- Right on Route 180.
- At flashing light, right on Route 17.
- Ride Route 17 through Brunswick and cross bridge over Potomac to Virginia (Route 17 becomes Route 287 south).

- Right on Route 673.
- Left on Route 690.
- Near Hillsboro, right on Route 9.
- Left on Route 719.
- Left on old Route 7.
- Return to Purcellville via Round Hill.

Not far from David Brown's weekend retreat, the area around the confluence of the Shenandoah and the Potomac rivers was hotly contested during the Civil War. Abolitionist John Brown's raid on Harpers Ferry helped precipitate the conflict. In 1862 Stonewall Jackson captured the town, much to the embarrassment of Abe Lincoln. Today most of the town has been preserved as a national park, with shops and historical exhibits installed in the old buildings. Founded in 1733, the town offers views of the surrounding rivers and mountains. (Thomas Jefferson called the vista of the two rivers meeting "one of the most stupendous scenes in nature.")

Just to the north, Antietam National Battlefield Park commemorates the war's bloodiest day of fighting. On September 17, 1862, some 23,000 of the blue and gray soldiers were killed or wounded. The battle ended in a draw, with the Southerners denied the tactical victory they hoped would end the war. The 6.5-mile one-way loop around the park is perfect for cyclists—providing they are feeling reverent. The last time I was there, a group of Civil War re-enactors, authentically dressed down to their eyeglasses, were solemnly setting up camp and preparing artillery as though they were about to charge into battle. They were living in old canvas tents and stoking pit fires, for this was November.

Other highlights of an Antietam tour include the West Woods, where Union forces lost 2,200 troops in thirty minutes; the homespun Dunker Church on disputed high ground; and Bloody Lane, no explanation needed. On the much less grisly side, you can turn off Route 65 for a visit to the Piper Farmhouse, an officer's headquarters during the battle. The 1843 log structure was recently restored as a bed-and-breakfast with kitchen privileges and reasonable rates. Staying overnight will give you more time to explore the upper reaches of the C & O Canal and, just across the river, the college burg of Shepardstown, West Virginia, which once thrived on mills and now thrives on antiques.

Antietam's historic sites are all mixed in with private farms and houses. This has caused some alarm, as preservationists charge that development will ruin this hallowed ground. So the battle for Antietam Creek has not been decided yet.

The region is fewer than 60 miles from central Washington, D.C., but at times it seems several worlds away. At least once a year the Potomac Area Chapter of American Youth Hostels sponsors guided rides out to Harpers Ferry. It's the easiest way I know of to cycle through three states in one day.

Bicycling Organizations in the D.C. Area

Bicycle Federation of America
1506 21st Street N.W.
Suite 200
Washington, D.C. 20036
(202) 463–6622

National nonprofit group that promotes safe bicycle use.

Potomac Chapter of American Youth Hostels
1108 K Street N.W.
Washington, D.C. 20005
(202) 783–4943

Local chapter of national group runs bike trips of one day or more, operates downtown youth hostel and bike/outdoors shop, plans rides to other hostels in the region.

Potomac Pedalers Touring Club
Box 23601, L'Enfant Plaza Station
Washington, D.C. 20026
(202) 363–8687

With more than 50,000 members, the Potomac Pedalers Club is the largest recreational cycling organization in the Washington area. The group runs weekly rides and tours, published in their monthly newsletter, "Pedal Patter."

Washington Area Bicyclist Association
818 Connecticut Avenue N.W.
Suite 300
Washington, D.C. 20006
(202) 872–9830

A group that advocates improved trails and routes for bicycle commuters. Also operates a warehouse for maps and cycling books.

Regional Conservation Groups

Audubon Naturalist Society
8940 Jones Mill Road
Chevy Chase, MD 20815
(301) 652–9188

Local environmental organization that offers many educational programs.

Potomac Appalachian Trail Club
118 Park Street S.E.
Vienna, VA 22180
(703) 242–0315

Local nonprofit group dedicated to creating and preserving hiking trails in the Mid-Atlantic region.

Maps to Obtain

ADC's Washington Area Bike Map. Compiled by Metropolitan Washington Council of Governments. $6.95. Available at bookstores and newsstands.

Arlington, Virginia, Bikeway Map and Guide. Published by the Arlington County Department of Public Works. Free. Contact Public Works Planning Division, No. 1 Court House Plaza, 2100 North Clarendon Boulevard, Arlington, VA 22201, (703) 358–3681.

D.C. Bikeways. Series of eight maps published by the city. $3.00. Includes pamphlet, "Getting Around Washington by Bicycle." Write to

D.C. Bicycling Coordinator, 2000 Fourteenth Street N.W., Washington, D.C. 20009.

Maryland Bicycle Touring Map. Free. Available from Office of Tourism Development, 45 Calvert Street, Annapolis, MD 21401.

Station Masters: A Comprehensive Guide to Metrorail Station Neighborhoods. Published by Bowring Cartographic. $3.95. Available at bookstores.

Trails in Montgomery County Parks. Available for $2.00 at most county parks, golf courses, and recreation areas. Contact Maryland National Capital Parks and Planning Commission (MNCPPC), 8787 Georgia Avenue N.W., Silver Spring, MD 20910, (301) 495–2525.

Virginia Atlas and Gazetteer. Published by DeLorme Mapping Company. Includes topographic maps, hike/bike trails, canoeing areas. $12.95. Available at bookstores.

Washington, D.C., and Vicinity Street Map. Published by ADC. $8.95. Available at bookstores.

W & OD R.R. Regional Park Trail Guide. Free. Contact Northern Virginia Regional Park Authority, 5400 Ox Road, Fairfax Station, VA 22039, (703) 352–5900. Also available from the W & OD Trail office at (703) 729–0596.

Suggested Reading

Applewhite, E. J. *Washington, Itself: An Informal Guide to the Capital of the United States*. New York: Knopf, 1981.

Choukas-Bradley, Melanie, and Polly Alexander. *City of Trees: The Complete Field Guide to the Trees of Washington, D.C*. Baltimore: The Johns Hopkins Press, 1987.

Colbert, Judy and Ed. *Virginia: Off the Beaten Path*. Fourth edition. Old Saybrook, CT: The Globe Pequot Press, 1995.

Federal Writers' Project. *The WPA Guide to Washington, D.C.* New York: Pantheon Books, 1983.

Goode, James M. *The Outdoor Sculpture of Washington, D.C.* Washington, D.C.: Smithsonian Institution Press, 1974.

Hahn, Thomas F. *Towpath Guide to the C & O Canal*. Freemansburg, PA: American Canal Society, 1980.

Halle, Louis J. *Spring in Washington*. New York: Atheneum Publishers, 1963.

Helfer, Chuck and Gail. *Chuck and Gail's Favorite Rides*. Takoma Park, MD: Cycleways, 1992.

Highsmith, Carol, and Ted Landphair. *Pennsylvania Avenue: America's Main Street*. Washington, D.C.: AIA Press, 1988.

Pratson, Frederick. *Guide to Washington D.C. and Beyond*. Old Saybrook, CT: The Globe Pequot Press, 1989.

Smith, Kathryn Schneider, ed. *Washington at Home: An Illustrated History of Neighborhoods in the Nation's Capital*. Washington, D.C.: Columbia Historical Society, 1988.

Wilds, Claudia. *Finding Birds in the National Capital Area*. Washington, D.C.: Smithsonian Institution Press, 1983.

Wurman, Richard Saul. *Washington, D.C. Access: The Capital Guide to the Capital City*. Los Angeles: Access Press, 1989.

Bicycle Rental Centers
in the D.C. Area

Bicycle Exchange, 1506 C Belle View Boulevard, Alexandria, VA (on the Mount Vernon Bike Trail). (703) 768–3444.

Big Wheel Bikes, 1034 33rd Street N.W., Washington, D.C. (202) 337–0254. All types of bikes.

City Bikes, 2501 Champlain Street N.W., Washington, D.C. (near Rock Creek Bike Path). (202) 265–1564. City and mountain bikes.

Fletcher's Boat House, 4940 Canal Road N.W., Washington, D.C. (202) 244–0461. One- and three-speed bikes. Seasonal.

Metropolis Bike & Scooter, Inc. On Capitol Hill: 709 8th Street S.E., Washington, D.C. (202) 543–8900. In Arlington: 4056 South 28th Street (The Village at Shirlington), Arlington, VA. (703) 671–1700. All types of bikes.

Proteus Bikes, 7945 MacArthur Boulevard, Cabin John, MD. (301) 229–5900. All types of bikes and bike trailers.

Spinnaker 'n' Spoke, at the Washington Sailing Marina (Daingerfield Island), on the Mount Vernon Bike Path. (703) 548–9027. One- and three-speed bikes. Seasonal.

Swain's Lock, about 1 mile west of Great Falls on the C & O Canal. One-speed bikes; tandems. Seasonal.

Thompson Boat Center, Rock Creek Parkway & Virginia Avenue N.W., Washington, D.C. (202) 333–4861. One- and three-speed bikes. Seasonal.

Washington Bike Center (Reston Town Center), 11932 Democracy Drive, Reston, VA. (703) 742–7775. All kinds of bikes.

About the Author

Michael Leccese is a writer and editor for *Landscape Architecture* magazine. His articles on architecture, travel, and the environment have appeared in such publications as the *Washington Post, Historic Preservation,* and the *Miami Herald.* He is also the author of Globe Pequot's *Short Bike Rides in Colorado* and the coauthor of *The Bicyclist's Sourcebook: The Ultimate Directory of Cycling Information* (Woodbine House, 1991). An advocate of bicycle commuting, he has toured much of Europe and the United States on two wheels.

Also of Interest from The Globe Pequot Press

The Best Bike Rides In The Mid-Atlantic $12.95
Covering NY, PA, NJ, DE, MD, WV, and D.C.

Quick Escapes from Washington, D.C. $13.95
25 Weekend Trips from the Nation's Capital

Guide to The Jersey Shore $12.95
From Sandy Hook to Cape May

*Day Trips, Getaway Weekends, and Vacations
In The Mid-Atlantic States* $16.95
11 Itineraries that cover the Mid-Atlantic region

Other titles in this Series:

Short Bike Rides on Cape Cod, Nantucket and the Vineyard $9.95

Short Bike Rides in Central and Western Massachusetts $12.95

Short Bike Rides in Connecticut $9.95

Short Bike Rides in Eastern Massachusetts $14.95

Short Bike Rides in and around Los Angeles $11.95

Short Bike Rides in Michigan $10.95

Short Bike Rides in New Jersey $9.95

Short Bike Rides in Rhode Island $10.95

Short Bike Rides in and around San Francisco $ 9.95

Short Bike Rides in Western Washington $12.95

Short Bike Rides in Colorado $10.95

Available from your bookstore or directly from the publisher.
For a catalogue or to place an order, call toll free, 24 hours a day,
1-800-243-0495, or write to The Globe Pequot Press, P.O. Box 833,
Old Saybrook, Connecticut 06457-0833.